We love the Lakes. It is Britain's favourite national park. and so much more. landscape that has  great writers and artists, launch thousands of walks and spawne memories for generations of fam...

And what's not to like? The natural landscape, the outdoor activities, the great local food, the soft-sand beaches, the cool campsites, the wide-open skies, the fact that people make you feel instantly at home. Good times.

With all of us keeping a tight check on our finances these days, holidays close to home are very much in vogue. The region is buzzing with things to do, many of which are inexpensive or even free. There are fantastic days out, family attractions and off-the-beaten-track escapes. But which one is right for your family?

This is where *Lake District with Kids* comes in. It offers a wealth of ideas to inspire and inform, a friendly word to pinpoint the smart option for small children, or a wise word on what might keep teenagers happy. It helps keep your costs down, but also identifies the best places to go when you want to treat the family to something a little bit special.

Award-winning travel writer **David Atkinson** (atkinsondavid.co.uk) is a freelance journalist based in Chester. He writes about travel for newspapers and magazines, including the *Observer*, *Wanderlust* and *Coast*, and writes the blog *Hit the North* about travel in the Northwest. More importantly, he is dad to four-year-old Maya, who joined him on some of the research trips for this book.

About the book

Lake District with Kids is like a Cumberland sausage: tasty, hearty and packed with local flavour. It's designed to help you explore one of the most diverse regions of Britain. On this page you'll find useful background information on getting the most out of the book, plus some important safety advice.

Beach safety

The 'FLAGS' code by the RNLI (rnli.org.uk/beachlifeguards) is a handy checklist for staying safe at the beach:
F Find the red and yellow flags and swim between them.
L Look at the safety signs.
A Ask a lifeguard for advice.
G Get a friend to swim with you.
S Stick your hand in the air and shout for help if you get into difficulty.

Tides & waves

• Always check local tide times. Tide tables also give information on tidal range which varies with the phases of the moon.
• Use bbc.co.uk/weather/marine/tides for precise tide times and details.
• Remember tides occur twice a day.
• Be careful not to get cut off by the tide when walking along the shore. Set off when the tide is on its way out and always keep an eye on it.
• Ensure children on the beach are not in danger of the tide or waves.

Family rates

Unless otherwise specified, family rates quoted in *Lake District with Kids* are for two adults and two children. Larger families should check if there are special deals.

Members' perks

Throughout Lake District with Kids, there are many properties, attractions and nature reserves that are free to members of English Heritage, the National Trust and the Royal Society for the Protection of Birds (RSPB). Family membership of these charities represents excellent value for money when travelling in Britain, and also helps to support conservation work.

English Heritage T0870-333 1182, english-heritage.org.uk. Annual membership £44/adult, including up to six children (under 19).

National Trust T0844-800 1895, nationaltrust.org.uk. Annual family membership £82 (two adults and their children or grandchildren under 18, under-fives free). Direct debit rate of £61.50 is available for the first year's membership.

RSPB T01767-693680, rspb.org.uk. For family membership (two adults and all children under 19) you can choose how much to give, although £51/year is the guideline. Members receive gifts and magazines.

Blue Flag awards

These are given for one season only and are subject to change.

Tourist boards

Details of tourist information and heritage centres are given in relevant chapters and in Grown-ups' stuff, page 182. The main site for information about Cumbria is golakes.co.uk.

Symbol Key

Beaches
- Blue Flag award
- Café/pub/restaurant
- Beach shop
- Deckchairs
- Beach huts
- Water sports
- Amusement arcade
- Lifeguards (summer)
- Dogs allowed all year
- Toilets nearby
- Car park nearby
- Warning!

Campsites
- Tents
- Caravans
- Shop
- Playground
- Picnic area
- Disabled facilities
- Dogs welcome
- Walk to beach
- Electric hook-up
- Family bathroom
- Baby care area
- Bike hire
- Café or takeaway van on site
- Campfires permitted

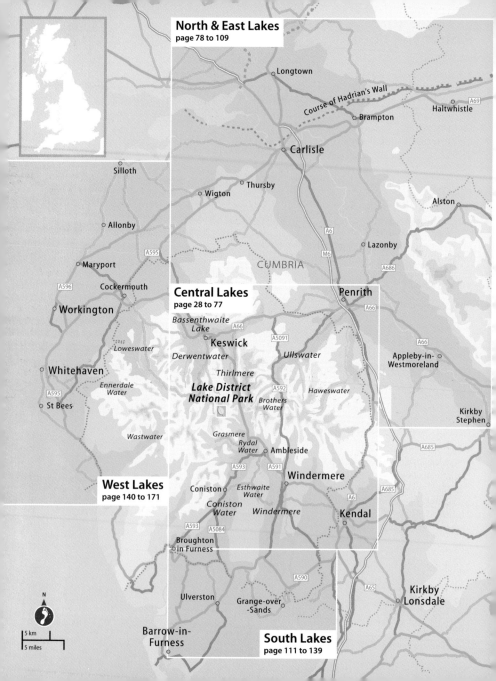

North & East Lakes
page 78 to 109

Longtown

Course of Hadrian's Wall

Haltwhistle
A69

Brampton

Carlisle

Silloth

Thursby

Wigton

Alston

Allonby

A595

Lazonby

Maryport

CUMBRIA

A686

A596

Cockermouth

Workington

Central Lakes
page 28 to 77

Penrith

A66

Bassenthwaite
Lake
A66

Keswick

A5091

Ullswater

Appleby-in-
Westmoreland

A66

Derwentwater

Thirlmere

Whitehaven

A595

Ennerdale
Water

St Bees

Loweswater

**Lake District
National Park**

A592

Haweswater

Kirkby
Stephen

Brothers
Water

Wastwater

Grasmere
Rydal
Water

Ambleside

A685

West Lakes
page 140 to 171

Coniston

A593

A591

Windermere

A685

Esthwaite
Water

Windermere

A66

Coniston
Water

Kendal

A6

A593

A5084

Broughton
in Furness

A590

A65

Ulverston

Grange-over
-Sands

Kirkby
Lonsdale

Barrow-in-
Furness

South Lakes
page 111 to 139

N

5 km
5 miles

Contents

Big days out
Aquarium of the Lakes
Lakeside 54
Bond Museum Keswick 59
Cumberland Pencil Museum
Keswick 59
Holker Hall & Gardens
Cark-in-Cartmel 124
Honister Slate Mine
Borrowdale 55
Lake District Coast Aquarium
Maryport 156
Lake District Visitor Centre
Brockhole 32
Muncaster Castle
Ravenglass 156
South Lakes Wild Animal
Park Dalton-in-Furness 126
Tullie House Carlisle 99

Action stations
Bigland Hall Equestrian
Newby Bridge 122
Coniston Water cycle trail
Coniston 46
Cumbrian Heavy Horses
Millom 152
Go Ape! Grizedale Forest Park 40
High Newton Trout Fishery
Grange-over-Sands 122
Stonetrail Holidays
Ravenstonedale 90
Ventures West Maryport 152
Via Ferrata & Zip Honister Slate
Mine 46
West Coast Karting
Maryport 152
Windermere Canoe Bowness-
on-Windermere 44

Living history
Birdoswald Roman Fort
Brampton 95
Brantwood Coniston 54
Carlisle Castle Carlisle 101
Castlerigg Stone Circle
Keswick 33
Hill Top Hawkshead 55
Holker Hall Cark-in-Cartmel 124
Lanercost Priory Brampton 95
Ravenglass Roman Bath
House Ravenglass 146
Rydal Mount Grasmere 51
Wordsworth House and
Garden Cockermouth 157

Fun & free
Complete the Ullswater circuit
walk 85
Find Ennerdale Water 144
Visit the Dock Museum, Barrow-
in-Furness 127
Follow Coniston's town trail 33
Hike the Tarn Hows trail 36
Marvel at Watbarrow Point,
Windermere 63
Spot red squirrels in Whinlatter
Forest Park 32
Run free at Bitts Park, Carlisle 84
Savour Britain's favourite view,
Wasdale Head 144
Walk the Ulverston
Town Trail 130

Rainy day activities
Augill Little Cooks Kirkby
Stephen 90
Beatrix Potter Gallery
Hawkshead 58
The Beacon Whitehaven 156
Brewery Arts Centre
Kendal 74
Center Parcs Whinfell Forest
Penrith 105

Lakeland Climbing Centre
Kendal 46
Lakeland Motor Museum
Backbarrow 129
Laurel & Hardy Museum
Ulverston 133
The Rheged Centre Penrith 84
Upfront Gallery & Puppet
Theatre Penrith 99

Wild about wildlife
Derwentwater Site of Special
Scientific Interest Keswick 35
Grizedale Forest Park
Hawkshead 38
Hodbarrow Nature Reserve
Bowness on Solway 117
Low Furness Peninsula
Ulverston 118
St Bees Head
near Whitehaven 147
Solway Coast Discovery
Centre Silloth 160
Talkin Tarn Country Park
Brampton 82
Trotters World of Animals
Bassenthwaite 59
Walby Farm Park Carlisle 101
Whinlatter Forest Park
Keswick 153

Perfect pitches
Cartmel Camping & Caravan
Park Cartmel 134
Castlerigg Hall Caravan and
Camping Park Keswick 64
Low Wray Ambleside 64
Dalegarth Campsite
Cockermouth 164
Fisherground Campsite
Eskdale Valley 164
Full Circle yurts Rydal 65
Great Langdale Campsite
Langdale Valley 65

Lowther Holiday Park
Penrith 104
Park Cliffe Camping and Caravanning Estate
Windermere 64
Ullswater Caravan, Camping and Marine Park Penrith 104

Cool rides
Hadrian's Wall Country Bus 95
Keswick Launch Keswick 44
Lakeside and Haverthwaite Railway Lakeside 55
Platty+ Derwentwater 49
Ravenglass & Eskdale Railway Ravenglass 154
Steam yacht *Gondola*
Coniston 44
Tandem Paragliding
Keswick 49
Ullswater Steamers
Glenridding 93
Windermere Lake Cruises
Bowness-on-Windermere 44
Windermere Marina Village
Bowness-on-Windermere 66

Lake District highs
Climb Catbells, Keswick 48
Eat at Lucy's on a Plate, Ambleside 74
Build sandcastles on Allonby Beach 146
Play with spring lambs at Shacklabank Farm, Sedbergh 106
Pose for a picture next to the statue of Laurel & Hardy, Ulverston 133
Go pony trekking on the fells 90
Jump aboard La'al Ratty steam train 154
Walk a section of the Hadrian's Wall Path National Trail 91

Toast marshmallows on a campfire 164
Stop off at Tebay Motorway Service Station 102

Ace cafés
The Apple Pie Ambleside 71
Farrer's Tea & Coffee House
Kendal 72
Gillam's Ulverston 137
Good Taste Keswick 72
Hazelmere Café
Grange-over-Sands 137
Merienda Cockermouth 169
No 15 Penrith 109
The Watermill Gleaston 108
Wilf's Café Staveley 74
Yew Tree Farm Coniston 70

Local goodies
Bread Staff of Life, Kendal 71
Cheese The Lake District Creamery, Wigton 168
Cumberland sausage Richard Woodall, Waberthwaite 137
Gingerbread Sarah Nelson's Gingerbread Shop, Grasmere 70
Kendal Mint Cake 1657 Chocolate Shop, Kendal 72
Potted shrimps Ray's Shrimps, Silloth 168
Real Ale Hawkshead Brewery, Stavely 75
Rum Butter The Rum Story, Whitehaven 170
Sticky Toffee Pudding Village Shop, Cartmel 136
Trout Bessy Becks Trout Farm 90

Pony trekking
near Coniston.

Family favourites

Feather Down Farms

Feather Down farm tents lead the herd when it comes to luxury camping. Found on working farms around the UK, the winning formula remains simple: cool camping plus effortless immersion in real farm life. Behind the flap of these canvas creations is everything you need for a cosy family break, including a wood-burning stove, oil lanterns and private bedrooms, incorporating a secret cubbyhole for kids. There's no electricity and the car is parked out of sight in the farmyard, so the distractions of Sat Nav and television are dispensed with in favour of the calming rhythm of farm life.

The Lakeland representative of this national group is Howbeck Lodge Farm, set at the foot of the Skiddaw range in the heart of the Lake District National Park. It is about 12 miles from Keswick and two miles from the village of Caldbeck. Howbeck is a traditional family sheep and beef farm with over 300 acres. The tents are located in a field with a stream, overlooking a small wood, making red squirrels, foxes, roe deer and badgers the campsite's only neighbours.

In keeping with other Feather Down sites, Howbeck Lodge's facilities include clay ovens for self-catered bread and pizzas, an open invitation to collect eggs from the henhouse, and an honesty shop. The latter, housed in the top of a converted hog house, offers home-made soups, fresh produce, ready meals and jams. The showers are at ground level, below the shop; each tent has its own private toilet.

Guests are encouraged to muck in with farm life – from simply saying hello to the animals in the paddock to more hands-on activities, such as bottle-feeding the orphan lambs in spring. Otherwise, kids can hire bikes for a cycle ride, play hide and seek, or build a den in the woods. In the evening, it's a matter of cooking around the stove the old-fashioned way before settling down to bedtime stories by candlelight and sweet dreams of another day on the farm.

Wigton, CA7 8JN, T01697-478206, featherdown.co.uk.
Apr-Oct £395-795/week, £275-575/weekend,
£195-525/midweek (Mon-Fri).

Pod camping

Camping these days needn't be about huddling against the gale with a Calor gas stove and a tin of baked beans. Camping has a new secret weapon to beat the downpours of a Great British summer while still keeping the expense down: pods. These barrel-like pods look like a cross between a garden shed and something you might have assembled from a flat-pack from IKEA, but they are ideal for a spot of 'glamping'. And kids will love the idea of sleeping in their very own secret den.

The Camping and Caravanning Club's Eskdale site was the first in the UK to offer the pods as an alternative to canvas, and the initiative proved an instant hit. Today, pods are springing up at campsites all around Cumbria. The National Trust has three sites for pods: Great Langdale, Wasdale and Low Wray (the latter suitable for up to two adults and three children). There are also three pods within the Grizedale Forest Park, while the Quiet Site near Ullswater has a quiet pod handy for the Quiet Bar.

The pods are a greener alternative to traditional camping and offer a more comfortable camping experience. A wooden-framed structure, insulated with sheep's wool and tiled with weatherproof slates, they keep out the wet and the cold. Inside, the pods are functional. Most can accommodate two adults comfortably, or a family with two small kids at a squeeze. There's plenty of headroom and enough space to swing a toddler – just. Most of them come with two camp beds, two folding chairs and a folding table; some have heaters. They all have lockable French windows, leading onto a deck, so you can keep your belongings secure. You need to bring pillows, sleeping bags and towels.

Camping and Caravanning Club, T0845-130 7633, campingand caravanningclub.co.uk/eskdale-camping-pods.
Grizedale Campsite and Riding Centre, T01229-860208, grizedale-camping.co.uk.
National Trust camping pods, T01539 463862, campsite.bookings@nationaltrust.org.uk.
The Quiet Site, T07768-727016, thequietsite.co.uk.
Prices typically around £40/night (sleeping two to four).

See also **pod.info** for more pod camping locations.

Center Parcs

Adults can be sniffy about Center Parcs, but for kids nothing beats a holiday at one of these action-packed woodland villages, where boredom – like your car – is left at the entrance when you arrive.

Of the four forest village locations around the UK, Cumbria is represented by Center Parcs Whinfell Forest, a 400-acre woodland site set among Norwegian spruce trees. The range of activities on offer is dizzying and, to be frank, not cheap for families on a tight budget. They range from paint ball to a teddy bears' picnic and include all the kids' favourites such as pony trekking, quad biking, kayaking and windsurfing. But the combination of water, woodland and wildlife will keep the most fidgety of children occupied from first thing in the morning to last thing at night. And, if the weather lets you down, fear not. There are lots of indoor activities to beat those soggy half-term blues.

One tip: bring your swimming gear and make the Subtropical Swimming Paradise, essentially a mini Eden Project with water chutes, your best friend. It is free to all guests, and the perfect place to teach kids to swim and build their water confidence in a safe environment. Whinfell Forest is also strong on aerial activities, with climbing walls and abseiling a superb way to foster children's self-confidence. The sense of making a contribution to conservation comes across well, too, with ranger trails, nature walks and birdwatching all helping children develop an interest in the natural world.

But it's not just about the kids at Center Parcs. Whinfell Forest offers a good range of options for eating out and going for a quiet drink. The various cafés and restaurants are all very family friendly, but with babysitting services available daily (at extra charge), parents can also grab some quality time together as part of the holiday. Or even head to the Indonesian-style Aqua Sana Spa for an indulgent treatment or two. (Prices correct at time of going to press.)

Whinfell, nr Penrith, CA10 2DW, T0844-826 6266, centerparcs.co.uk/villages/whinfell. Year round from £239 (off peak) and £519 (peak)/short break for a two-bedroom villa (sleeps four).

Luxury hotels

Going posh with kids is not easy. You have to find a luxury hotel without pretensions, one where child-friendly doesn't mean, "We put up with it, but don't expect us to like it."

Is there anything out there to fit the bill? Well, actually, yes. If you like a pampering massage and a fluffy bathrobe after a muddy fell walk, the Lake District has plenty of luxury hotels, including several that are surprisingly welcoming of children.

They've got the spa, the stunning suites (with interconnecting rooms, of course) and the hugely quaffable wine list. But what sets these places apart form a bland corporate-chain hotel is the way staff aim to make children feel special too.

Some of them also offer family-oriented services such as babysitting. **Holbeck Ghyll**, Windermere, provides cots, high chairs and baby listening, and children under eight can have high tea at 1730, with babysitting available for later. **Armathwaite Hall**, near Keswick, runs activities during weekends and school holidays throughout the year as part of its Children's Country Club, plus there's free admittance to the adjoining Trotters World of Animals (see page 59). It also accommodates children under 12 free of charge when sharing with two adults.

Rothay Manor, Ambleside, offers a flexible choice of rooms, plus cots, fridges to store milk, and a baby-listening service. They also offer a high tea for children (£3-12) in the early evening. Look out, too, for the **Swan Hotel** and **Lakeside Hotel**, both in Newby Bridge, the former with a fantastic selection of children's games and books as well as milk and cookies before bed.

Armathwaite Hall, Bassenthwaite, nr Keswick, CA12 4RE, T01768-776551, armathwaite-hall.com.
Holbeck Ghyll, Windermere, LA23 1LU, T01539-432375, holbeckghyll.com.
Lakeside Hotel, Newby Bridge, Lake Windermere, T01539-530001, LA12 8AT, lakesidehotel.co.uk.
Rothay Manor, Ambleside, LA22 0EH, T01539-433605, rothaymanor.co.uk.
The Swan Hotel, Newby Bridge, LA12 8NB, T01539-531681, swanhotel.com

Lakeside lodges

Specialist self-catering operator Hoseasons operates over 200 lodges around the UK. Within Cumbria, four parks offer lakeside lodges that are ideal for families looking for a rustic break. Unlike some sites, the parks are not located in isolated areas, but close to towns, including Kendal, Windermere and Ambleside. As such, they offer a good-value break within easy driving distance of the region's key attractions.

The real beauty of a Hoseasons' lodge, however, is the flexibility of having your own well-equipped self-catering cabin combined with top-notch on-site facilities and a superb natural setting.

The facilities on the six sites vary, and it's best to choose a site that suits the age of your children. White Cross Bay, for example, has been given Hoseasons' Active Breaks status and is ideal for school-age children. It offers an indoor swimming pool, a children's playground and boating excursions on nearby Windermere.

Bassenthwaite Lakeside Lodges, on the other hand, is listed as a 'peace and quiet' location and therefore better suited to parents with babies who are seeking rest and relaxation but still want good facilities to hand. These lodges make a good base for touring the wider region, while a well-stocked lending library of books and DVDs on site mean it's perfectly possible just to hide away and chill. Some of the Hoseasons sites have lodges equipped with their own hot tubs for a relaxing alfresco soak.

All the lodges have a modern fitted kitchen (with a microwave oven), satellite television and a patio with garden furniture. Bed linen and towels are also provided. Some lodges have a washing machine, others a communal launderette; some sites have a clubhouse for family meals and snacks. See individual properties for more details. Cots and high chairs can be hired (from £10/week each) and pets are also welcome (from £25/week).

Hoseasons, T0844-8471356, hoseasons.co.uk/lodges. Prices from £232/week (sleeps four) at White Cross Bay, Windermere, and from £385/week at Bassenthwaite Lakeside Lodges. Check online for promotional deals.

Yurts

They know a thing or two about camping in Mongolia. The traditional Mongolian yurt (or *ger*, as it is called there), designed to be dismantled and carried on camels or yaks, consists of a circular wooden frame with a multi-layered felt and canvas cover for superb insulation. Recently, the makeshift homes of nomadic yak herders have caught on as the latest cool-camping trend and the yurt has come to the heart of the English Lakes.

Yurts make a surprisingly cosy base for a family break and kids will love the idea of sleeping in their very own forest hideaway. Parents, too, will be pleasantly surprised to find that the design of yurts keeps one warm in winter and cool in summer.

Yurts can normally accommodate up to six people and come equipped with a wood-burning stove, lanterns, rugs and comfortable beds, offering a touch of home comforts away from home. Hire includes the usual camping equipment, a gas hob, cooking utensils, and lots of candles for bedtime stories. But don't expect an en suite toilet or plug-and-play electricity.

One Cumbrian company specializing in yurts is **Full Circle**, which keeps a small group of yurts at its site at Rydal, near Ambleside. The site has a tap for fresh water, picnic facilities and hammocks. The National Trust's **Great Langdale Campsite** near Ambleside also has two fully equipped 18ft-diameter yurts, with comfortable beds (cotton sheets, pillow cases and duvets provided) and Moroccan lanterns. The Great Langdale site also has a family area and a play area for children. Whichever you choose, families will learn that those Mongolians had the right idea all along.

Full Circle, T07975-671928, lake-district-yurts.co.uk. Year round from £265/week off-peak and £295/week peak season.
Great Langdale Campsite, T01539-463862, langdale.camp@nationaltrust.org.uk. Mar-early Jan, from £295/off-peak, £325 peak season.

First-class male

John Cunliffe's tales of village life in the Greendale Valley for Postman Pat and his faithful cat, Jess, were inspired by the sleepy Kentmere Valley, near Kendal. Pat became the unlikely star of a popular BBC TV series and he still plies his trade today, albeit in the new setting of Pencaster (a double for Penrith, perhaps?) and has been armed with a Sat Nav for his van.

Every year in September, the steam-powered Ravenglass & Eskdale Railway becomes the Greendale Railway for a weekend, with a Postman Pat-themed party awaiting the arrival of the trains at Dalegarth station.

The Museum of Lakeland Life in Kendal (see page 57) also has a room dedicated to Postman Pat, where young children can learn more about the character and also post letters to his creator, John Cunliffe.

Books set in the Lakes

• *The Eagle of the Ninth*, Rosemary Sutcliff. A historical adventure set in Hadrian's Wall country. The book, published in 1954, was recently made into a film, to be released in 2010.
• *Swallows and Amazons*, Arthur Ransome. The nautical adventures of the Walker and Blackett families.
• *No Boats on Bannermere*, Geoffrey Trease. Follow what the Melbury family get up to when they move to the Lake District.
• *The Tale of Peter Rabbit*, Beatrix Potter. Probably the best loved of Potter's stories.

Play the signs of adventure game

Keep your eyes peeled. There's been an outbreak of renegade road signs around the Lakeland peaks. In fact, the 10 offbeat 'Signs of Adventure' were created by Cumbria Tourism to promote adventures in the great outdoors. Spotting the signs has become the new I-Spy for family holidays in the region.

The signs show passing paragliders, bunny-hopping mountain-bikers, drifting hot-air balloons and a climber taking on a rock fall, as well as wild horse-riders and rapid-riding kayakers, amongst others. The tourism team even lugged one sign all the way up Scafell.

One of the most striking signs gives the Elderly People traffic sign, made in 1981, a 21st-century makeover – a reinvigorated elderly couple hiking up a hill with backpacks and Nordic walking poles. The sign is located near the aptly named Old Man of Coniston.

The long-term plan is to transfer the signs to an outdoor exhibition of public artworks, possibly at Grizedale Forest Park (see page 38).

More from golakes.co.uk/signsofadventure, or view them on Facebook at facebook.com/pages/The-Lake-District-Cumbria/66266195119?v=photos&viewas=0.

Animal antics

The recent arrivals at Trotters World of Animals (CA12 4 RD, T017687-76239, trottersworld.com) near Bassenthwaite Lake are set for a life as TV stars. When the UK's only breeding pair of Canadian Lynx gave birth to a set of cubs during summer 2009, a film crew from TV's Channel 5 were at the park filming with Michaela Strachan. The cubs went on to feature in the TV series, *Michaela's Animal Road Trip*. Esther, their keeper, became the de facto agent to the lynx cubs and now gives a talk daily at 1530, including the chance for children to ask questions about the rare animals. The cubs are just one of the recent additions to the wildlife park. Others include Asian Fishing Cat kittens, a new zebra stallion and a baby lemur called Sprite.

Do the hokey pokey

The first water ices in Europe went on sale in Paris and Florence in the early 1660s, with ices made from sweetened milk arriving in Naples soon afterwards. Ice cream made its British debut at a banquet for the Feast of St George at Windsor Castle in 1671. Ice cream was originally called hokey pokey, from the vendors cry of "Ecco un poco" (try a sample). Cumbria is home to some great artisan ice cream producers.

Five of the best are:

Windermere Ice Cream and Chocolate Company
Windermere, LA23 2AL, T01539-47876, scoopchocice.com
Number of flavours: 32
Most unusual: wild cherry cheesecake
Open: year round Mon-Fri from 1000
Location: 15 mins from M6 junction 36, Bowness

Twentyman's
Allonby, CA15 6PE, T01900-881247
Number of flavours: 20
Most unusual: rhubarb and custard
Open: Apr-Sep daily 0900-2100, Oct-Mar daily 0900-1900

Location: M6 junction 40, then A66 to Cockermouth and A594 for coast road

Hartley's Ice Cream
Egremont, CA22 2AW, T01946-820456
Number of flavours: 60-plus
Most unusual: honeycomb crunch
Open: year round daily 1100-1900
Location: M6 junction 41, then A66 to Bridgefoot and A595 to Egremont

English Lakes Ice Cream
Kendal, LA9 6NT, T01539-721211, lakesicecream.com
Number of flavours: 40
Most unusual: toffee butterscotch
Open: year round Mon-Fri 0900-1600, Sat 0900-1230
Location: M6 junction 39, then A6 following signs for Shap

Abbott Lodge Jersey Ice Cream
Penrith, CA10 2HD, T01931-712720, abbottlodgejerseyicecream.co.uk
Number of flavours: 30
Most unusual: trifle
Open: Easter-Oct daily 1100-1700, Nov-Apr closed Mon and Fri
Location: M6 junction 40, then A6 for Shap and through Clifton Village

❷ The average number of licks to polish off a single scoop of ice cream cone is 50.

Take a waterfall walk

There are over 150 waterfalls in the Lake District. They are one of the most spectacular features of a mountainous area and because they are often hidden away in wooded gorges they can be a perfect outdoors escape on a rainy day. Experiencing the roar of the cascading water is one of the best ways to get a taste for the great outdoors.

Amongst the pick of the waterfall walks are the following:

· Aira Force, Ullswater
The most popular falls in the Lakes, this magnificent 21 m multiple fall has bridges above and below for viewing.

· The Howk, Caldbeck
A deep limestone gorge, the geology of which is unique in the Lake District.

· Launchy Ghyll, Thirlmere
A long set of thunderous falls and cascades with close access from paths and a footbridge.

· Rydal Falls, Rydal Water
A whole chain of cascades set in a deep, wooded valley, leading to the impressive falls.

· Scale Force
The highest falls in the Lakes at 52 m and hidden in a deep cleft.

· Tom Gill Falls, Tarn Hows
A rewarding set of falls and cascades accessible with a short stroll from the National Trust car park.

Join the Cumbria Wildlife Trust

Herdwick sheep, Langdale.

The Cumbria Wildlife Trust (T01539-816300, cumbriawildlifetrust.org.uk) manages 40 Lakeland nature reserves, including ancient woodland, flower-rich meadows and wetland habitats. They are refuges for threatened plants and animals, and unspoilt places for a back-to-nature visit. According to Simon King of BBC *Springwatch* and *Autumnwatch*, "There is no other body I know that represents the nation but at the same time represents your local patch on a very personal level."

By joining the Trust, you can attend Wildlife Watch days, a wildlife club running family events for all ages, whereby kids are encourage to muck in and get involved.

Six of the best sites managed by the Trust are as follows:
· Barkboot Lot near Keswick
· Clints Quarry near Egremont
· Dubbs Moss near Cockermouth
· Foulnety Island near Barrow-in-Furness
· Next Ness near Penrith
· Waitby Greenriggs near Kirkby Stephen

If you wannabe a record breaker...

Scafell and Scafell Pike.

'Dedication, dedication. That's what you need – if you want to be a record breaker,' according to the song. Alternatively, just head for Cumbria. They've got so many record breakers that it's like your very own walk-through copy of the *Guinness Book of Records*.

Here's a sample:
· The five highest peaks in England, namely Scafell Pike, Scafell, Helvellyn, Skiddaw and Bowfell

· The steepest road in England, namely the Hardknot Pass which has an overall gradient of 33%

· The deepest lake in England is Wastwater with a depth of 88.6 m

· The smallest church in England, St Olaf's at the head of the Wasdale Valley

· The best drive in Britain, according to Sat Nav company Garmin, is the A591 between Windermere and Keswick

· The world's tallest pencil is over 7.6 m long and housed at the Cumberland Pencil Museum in Keswick

Got your own favourite record breaker? Write in and tell us about it.

Take a stroll around Tarn Hows.

Where's woolly?

We all know that Cumbria is well known for its hardy Herdwick sheep. But there's a black sheep in every flock and Woolly, the hitchhiking Herdwick, has broken free of his pen at Fell Foot Farm, Little Langdale.

The reason? He wants to help children find the best of the Lake District for little ones like him – well, he is just 60 cm high. His website offers fun activities and top tips while his blog details his adventures while exploring Cumbria.

Shaggy-grey Woolly, who confesses a sheepish penchant for *One Man and His Dog* and Kendal mint cake, has compiled a Lake District quiz for kids and stars in a series of e-postcards. He also offers advice on some of his favourite family walks, such as a two-mile, pushchair-friendly circular stroll around Tarn Hows near Hawkshead, or a two-mile wildlife walk from Arnside Knott on the edge of Morecambe Bay.

Look out for Woolly on your own travels, and check out his website whereswoolly.co.uk for more details. You can even follow Woolly's blog at wheres-woolly.blogspot.com.

Make sticky toffee pudding

Cartmel (see page 136) is the home of Britain's best sticky toffee pudding. This easy recipe serves eight and takes less than one hour from start to serving.

Ingredients
200g dried dates, stoned and chopped
250ml black tea (not too strong)
½ tsp bicarbonate of soda
85g unsalted butter, softened
175g self-raising flour
1 tsp mixed spice
175g caster sugar
2 eggs, beaten

For the sauce
100g light muscovado sugar
100g unsalted butter
142 ml carton double cream

Method
❶ First heat the oven to 180°C or gas mark 4. Bring the dates and tea to the boil in a saucepan and cook for 3-4 minutes to soften the dates. Then stir in the bicarbonate of soda.

❷ Use an electric mixer to beat the butter and caster sugar until pale and creamy. Then beat in the beaten egg, flour and mixed spice. Fold in the date mixture and pour into a buttered ovenproof dish. Bake this for 30 minutes.

❸ To make the sauce, stir the sugar, butter and cream together in a pan over a low heat. Simmer until the sugar has dissolved and the sauce takes on a toffee-coloured hue.

❹ Finally, cut the pudding into squares and serve with the warm sauce and a scoop of vanilla ice cream. Yum!

Contents

Central Lakes

View towards
Ambleside from the
Drunken Duck Inn.

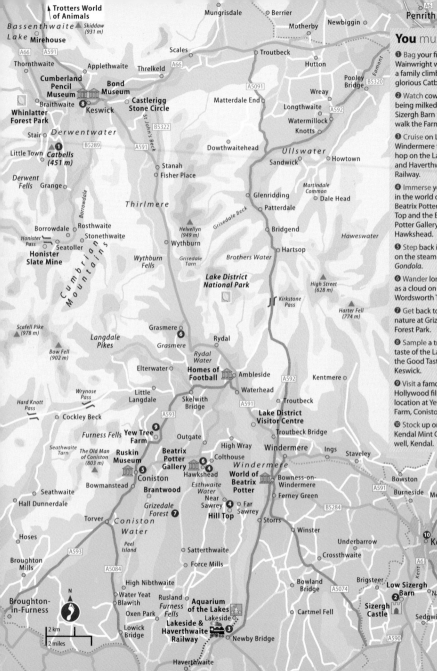

You must

❶ Bag your first Wainwright with a family climb up glorious Catbells.

❷ Watch cows being milked at Low Sizergh Barn then walk the Farm Trail.

❸ Cruise on Lake Windermere then hop on the Lakeside and Haverthwaite Railway.

❹ Immerse yourself in the world of Beatrix Potter at Hill Top and the Beatrix Potter Gallery, Hawkshead.

❺ Step back in time on the steam yacht *Gondola*.

❻ Wander lonely as a cloud on the Wordsworth Trail.

❼ Get back to nature at Grizedale Forest Park.

❽ Sample a true taste of the Lakes at the Good Taste Café, Keswick.

❾ Visit a famous Hollywood film location at Yew Tree Farm, Coniston.

❿ Stock up on Kendal Mint Cake in, well, Kendal.

Low Sizergh Barn, Kendal.

Now this is the Lakes. The majestic fells, the sweeping landscapes, the gentle rippling of the waters in the breeze. This is the Lakes that inspired the Romantic poets and the Sublime artists. It is also the part of the Lakes that has inspired so many family holidays since the Lake District National Park, one of Britain's first national parks, was established in 1951.

The Central Lakes may have the best developed infrastructure and the blockbuster attractions, but it also has the biggest crowds and longest traffic jams during peak periods. It's here that you'll see a coach full of tourists attempting to tackle a rural B-road on a drizzly afternoon while a queue of cars snakes wearily along behind it. The Central Lakes' popularity has led to its best-known towns and villages being referred to as 'honey pots'. So don't expect to be alone.

So, options then. Firstly, travel off season if possible. Much of the Central Lakes operates on a long season with many of the attractions and the majority of the places to stay and eat remaining open until December and then reopening again in mid-February. Otherwise, resign yourself to the fact this is the most popular part of the Lakes and get on with it. On the plus side, a visit in high season means heaps of activities for kids and usually better weather in which to enjoy the endless natural beauty, so that a day out doesn't have to burn a gaping hole in the budget.

Most of all, this region of Cumbria is the place to get out on the lakes and soak up the views from the water. Cumbria has 16 official lakes and most of them lie in the central region. So, whether it's a cruise on Coniston, water sports on Windermere or simply paddling in the tranquil shallows of Derwentwater, embrace the lakes themselves.

The names of the main destinations will already be familiar to most visitors. **Coniston**, with its links to the Campbell family, breakers of world water-speed records; **Windermere** for its boat trips; **Grasmere** for the legacy of William Wordsworth; **Hawkshead** for Beatrix Potter; and **Ambleside** with its ant trail of Gore-Tex jackets and stout walking boots.

It's not just about ticking off the honey pots, however. Take your time, enjoy the views, make it a leisurely lunch or picnic rather than a quick bite, and stop the car to let the children stretch their legs. Better still, leave the car behind altogether and take to the water or tackle the landscape on two wheels.

Out & about Central Lakes

Fun & free

Plan a Lakeland safari

Topping the list of wildlife to see are red squirrel and osprey, and neither should be too elusive. Red squirrels are found in forests throughout the Lake District (it's one of their major strongholds in England), but your best chance of seeing one is at Whinlatter Forest Park near Keswick (see page 153). From October to April, the visitor centre has a CCTV link to a red squirrel feeder, but if you think that's cheating try stalking the Squirrel Scurry Trail (maps are available from the visitor centre), keeping your eyes turned skyward for that tell-tale flash of ochre-red fur. Children completing the trail are given a squirrel mask or badge.

For further information on the Lake District's red squirrels,

contact Save our Squirrels (saveoursquirrels.org.uk).

During the summer months ospreys gain TV celebrity status at Whinlatter courtesy of live camera footage beamed from a nest at nearby Bassenthwaite Lake. Ospreys had not bred in England for over 150 years until they began using this site in 2001. RSPB volunteers at the Dodd Wood Viewpoint (rspb. org.uk/datewithnature, Apr-Aug daily 1000-1700) help visitors train telescopes on the raptors as they catch fish on the lake and carry food to their chicks.

The best way to reach both the viewpoint and Whinlatter Forest Visitor Centre is to hop on the Osprey Bus (74), a summer service around Bassenthwaite Lake from Keswick.

Whinlatter is England's only true mountain forest and it

offers plenty to keep all ages busy, from a choice of nature trails to learning about food webs and meeting the animals, including a badger.

Recent additions to the forest park are the high-wire treetops adventure Go Ape (see page 40) and new cycling trails, including the longest purpose-built mountain bike trail in the Lake District. More from forestry.gov.uk/forestry/infd-5gzlny.

Burn off that toddler energy

The tranquil riverside walk on the banks of the River Kent in Kendal makes for a lovely afternoon stroll, and is a great

---

Visit The Lake District Visitor Centre

Why? It's the perfect spot to ease yourself into the Lakes and dip your toes – literally if you like – in what the Lake District National Park has to offer. As well as exhibitions and displays, it has an information desk where you can plan walks and days out, while the terrace café commands views across the lake and fells. The grounds are brilliant for kids. They'll probably want to make a bee-line for the adventure playground or putting green, but try to coax them around the lakeshore and woodland walk first. During school holidays, children can take part in special activity days (some of which involve a small fee).

Where? Brockhole, between Troutbeck Bridge and Ambleside.

How? Gardens and adventure playground open year round dawn-dusk; centre, café and shop mid-Feb-Nov daily 1000-1700. Park in the pay-and-display car park, catch the 555 or 599 bus or take the launch from Ambleside Pier with Windermere Lake Cruises (see page 44).

Contact The Lake District Visitor Centre, LA23 1LJ, T01539-446601, lakedistrict.gov.uk.

place for toddlers to run off some steam. It's in the Kirkland district to the south of the town centre, the oldest part of Kendal, where green-and-white signs, made by the Kendal Civic Society, provide historical background. There is an adventure playground next to a small iron bridge over the river.

---

❷ The one-handed clock on the Moot Hall in Keswick is one of the oldest clocks in the country.

Browse Keswick's art scene
For families with an artistic bent, Keswick is a treasure trove of work by local artists and works inspired by the landscape of the Lakes. Older children may get inspiration for their next art project by browsing the following galleries (entry free). **Lee Chapman Gallery** (T01768-771188, leechapmangallery. co.uk) has paintings, sculpture, glassware, ceramics, furniture and jewellery. **Gallery 26 at 27** (T01768-772090, nelsonn. com) exhibits sculptures, paintings, photography, etchings and screen prints by the artist Nelsonn. **Northern Lights Gallery** (T01768-775402, northernlightsgallery. co.uk) features the work of over 80 northern artists. **Sharp Edge Gallery** (T01768-773788, sharpedgegallery. co.uk) shows work by Lake District artists. **Viridian Gallery** (T01768-771328, viridiangallery.

Count the stones

Legend has it that if you count the standing stones at Castlerigg Stone Circle, near Keswick, you'll never reach the same total twice. The 5000-year-old stone circle, set on a grassy plateau surrounded by a magnificent mountain panorama, is officially made up of 38 megaliths, plus an additional 10 that form a curious rectangle on one side of the ring. It is thought the stones were linked to the seasonal movements of the sun and moon. A larger, though less well-known, stone circle at Little Salkeld near Penrith is Long Meg and her Daughters (see page 108), said to be a coven of witches turned to stone for dancing on the Sabbath. Think twice about counting these stones – if you get the same number twice, the curse will be undone.

Castlerigg Stone Circle.

co.uk) also displays work by local artists, including the watercolourist Diane Gainey. **Thornthwaite Galleries** (nr Keswick, CA12 5SA, T01768-778248, thornthwaitegalleries. co.uk) exhibits paintings, sculpture, pottery, carvings and jewellery, mainly from Cumbria.

Take a village stroll
The village of Coniston may not have the immediate chocolate-box, bucolic charm of nearby Hawkshead or Grizedale, but it has a slew of short walks in the surrounding area and is a great spot to stretch little legs after a car journey.

The well-equipped tourist information office in Coniston (T01539-441533, conistontic. org), located in the pay-and-display car park, sells a useful little booklet called *Coniston Village Guide, Places of Interest and Short Walks*, for £1.

There's a lovely walk of about two miles to the head of the lake over easy terrain. Follow the Hawkshead road (B5285) out of the village, and pick up the footpath soon after the bridge. There are seats, toilets and a children's play area at the lake head, while the path is accessible to both pushchairs and wheelchairs. This is a good

Frost at the edge
of Derwentwater.

Cumbria Tourism classifies 16 major lakes in the Lake District, although only one, Bassenthwaite, is actually called a lake. The rest are waters, meres, or tarns. Each has its own charm and character. You can take boat trips on Windermere, Ullswater, Derwentwater and Coniston (see page 44), while water sports are available on many of the lakes (see page 49).

Derwentwater

At three miles long and one mile wide, Derwentwater is the third-largest of the Cumbrian lakes. It was joined to Bassenthwaite Lake until the silting up of the section west of Keswick. They are the only two lakes in the UK to contain the vendace – a species of fish dating from the last Ice Age – making Derwentwater a Site of Special Scientific Interest.

Unusually for the Lakes, it has four wooded islands: Derwent Island, St Herbert's Island, the largest and named after a hermit who once lived there, Lord's Island and Rampsholme, the smallest island. There is also a floating island that appears sporadically towards the end of summer. It consists of a mass of plant matter that rises to the surface on a cushion of methane gas.

In the 16th century Derwent Island was occupied by German miners working in the local lead industry, and later bought by Joseph Pocklington, a wealthy eccentric, who commissioned Derwent Island House in the Italianate style. He also built a collection of follies, including a mock church and a fort, and staged annual regattas and mock battles on the lake.

The National Trust now owns the island and lets it out to long-term tenants on the condition that they open the house to visitors each year.

There are many outstanding views over Derwentwater. Friar's Crag, a rocky pine-clad promontory near the northern end of the lake, provides superb views across the lake to Borrowdale. John Ruskin was moved to declare this to be one of the finest views in Europe. Nearby is a memorial to Canon Rawnsley, the former vicar of Crosthwaite church and one of the co-founders of the Trust in 1893.

Derwentwater is one of the richest lakes for wildlife and the easy going five- to six-mile walk around the lake is good for spotting greylag geese, alder leaf beetles and the locally scarce yellow wagtail.

Also recommended

Windermere

England's largest natural lake at 10 miles long, Windermere stretches from Waterhead, Ambleside, in the north to Lakeside in the south. It is surrounded by rolling hills and has a string of pretty towns and villages along the shore.

Coniston

At five miles long, Coniston is the third-largest lake after Windermere and Ullswater. It is best known for Donald Campbell's world water-speed record attempts in *Bluebird 7* (see page 36) and Arthur Ransome's series of children's books, *Swallows and Amazons*, inspired by locations around Coniston and Windermere. Ransome spent much of his childhood and part of his later life in the Lake District.

Grasmere

The lake lies to the south of the village and is a popular centre for gentle walks. The area was first highlighted by Wordsworth and other members of the Romantic Movement in the early 19th century.

Rydal Water

This is one of the smallest lakes in the national park but also one of its most popular on account of its Wordsworth connections. A series of steps leads up to Wordsworth's Seat, a rocky outcrop on the western side of the lake. The viewpoint is believed to have been one of the poet's favourite places.

Bassenthwaite Lake

Designated as a National Nature Reserve, this is the only true lake in the Lake District and home to the rare Vendace species of fish. There is an osprey viewing point (see page 32) at Dodd Wood on the east side of the lake.

Thirlmere

This clear lake provides the Manchester area with much of its water. Originally two lakes, it was turned into a reservoir at the end of the 19th century, submerging most of the village of Wythburn (its ruined buildings sometimes re-emerge during periods of drought). The A591 runs alongside its wooded shoreline, offering good views of the lake through the trees.

Esthwaite Water

This is a natural lake and one of the finest waters in the Lakes for pike and trout.

Elterwater

Known as the entrance to Great Langdale, Elterwater lies a few miles west of Ambleside and is hidden behind Loughrigg and Silver How.

place to spot local birdlife fluttering along the path.

For a longer walk, you can extend the lake head walk to Low Yewdale to make a two-hour trek. From the lake head, follow the Hawkshead road (B5285) to the first group of buildings then take a left and follow the track. Cross the Ambleside road and pass through an entrance in the wall opposite, then turn left and return to Coniston via the woods. This is a more demanding walk, but spectacular, and particularly special if your visit coincides with the spring flowers or autumn colours.

Whichever path you take, keep the Old Man of Coniston, the peak that dominates the village, as your reference point for navigation.

Hone your family's tree-spotting skills

While Monk Coniston Hall remains in private ownership, the estate is open access and home to the Monk Coniston Tree Trail. This is a delightful 2½-mile walk through the estate and a great way for kids to brush up on their tree-spotting skills. And don't

---

❷ Most trees have a common and a scientific name. These names can tell us a lot about the trees, such as what a tree looks like, where it comes from and even the name of the person who first discovered it.

worry, parents. If you can't tell your Copper Beech from your Coast Redwood, the National Trust produces a helpful leaflet that identifies the trees on the trail; ask for a copy in local tourist information offices.

The trail is marked 'Tarn Hows via Monk Coniston' and leads across farmland and garden paths, with some steep slopes. It has year-round appeal. Spring and early summer, for example, are ablaze with azaleas and rhododendrons, while autumn takes on the deep crimson hues of the Japanese maples, and winter is the best time to view the exotic conifers.

After exploring the tree collection, follow the footpath onto Tarn Hows (one mile), a man-made lake created in 1865 by the Marshall family, erstwhile country squires of the Monk Coniston Estate.

Park up at the head of Coniston Water, turning off the B525; the steam yacht *Gondola* (see page 45) stops at Monk Coniston jetty as part of its cruise around the lake.

Remember the Campbells

Before setting out from Coniston, seek out the Campbell Memorial, a stone seat and plaque on the village green across the road from the tourist information office. The simple, weather-beaten memorial marks the legacy of the Campbell family, who will be forever

Donald Campbell's grave, Coniston.

associated with the village of Coniston and Coniston Water.

Sir Malcolm Campbell and his son, Donald, used the lake as their base for successive attempts to break the world water-speed record. Sir Malcolm set a record of 141.7 mph in 1948 using the boat *Bluebird K4*. Donald went on to break numerous records in the remodelled *Bluebird K7*, but was tragically killed on Coniston on 4 January 1967, travelling at speeds of over 300 mph.

Today, the Lakeland Motor Museum in the South Lakes (see page 129) has a section devoted to the Bluebirds and the Campbells. Following the salvage of *Bluebird K4* from Coniston in 2001, the wreck was donated to the Ruskin Museum in Coniston (see page 58) and a new extension to the museum, due for completion in spring 2011, will house an expanded display about the Campbells and their legacy.

Coniston Water.

Grizedale Forest Park

et's face it: the honey pots of the Central Lakes are hardly an escape from it all in high season. But the Forestry Commission estate of Grizedale Forest Park, accessed from Hawkshead, offers a rare feeling of space and calm at the pulsing heart of the national park. If you go down to the woods today, the 6000-acre site offers action-packed days of walking, cycling and wildlife-watching.

Grizedale is a working forest but also makes for a gloriously off-the-beaten-track escape for a family-friendly activity break. There are myriad walking and biking trails, plus Go Ape, a high-wire adventure park. For less adrenaline-pumping pursuits, there is a trail of 80 outdoor sculptures (each numbered with its own sign) through the forest. Amongst the pieces of work on display are a giant xylophone and a towering forest spirit, who looms over Go Ape with a large axe in hand.

Get your bearings
Getting to Grizedale can test the nerve of less experienced drivers, especially if they are coming from the north. From the A591 (Ambleside), take the A593 and then B5286, heading south to bypass Hawkshead. From the edge of the forest, it's a two-mile drive along a narrow road with limited

❷ The terms softwood (eg pine, fir, spruce) and hardwood (eg oak, ash, beech) refer to the botanical origins of the timber and not its density or hardness.

passing. Coming from the south (M6, junction 36), follow the A590 to Haverthwaite, from where you'll see signposts for Grizedale Forest Park.

The on-site parking costs £4 per day; slightly confusingly, the turn for the main car park is beyond the turn-off to the visitor centre. There are four alternative car parks dotted around the park, some of which offer easier access to the walking trails (see page opposite).

Alternatively, the X30 Grizedale Wanderer bus (Apr-Nov) runs from Hawkshead via Grizedale and Lakeside and terminates at Haverthwaite. There are currently seven services per day and these connect with other routes, including the X35 Barrow–Kendal bus route, plus train and boat options from Lakeside (see page 55). For more details, consult Traveline (T0870-608 2608, travelcumbria.org.uk).

Essential information
Grizedale Forest Visitor Centre, LA22 0QJ, T01229-860010, forestry.gov.uk/grizedalehome, March-September 1000-1700, November-March 1000-1600

Hike the forest

There are eight way-marked and colour-coded (for difficulty) walking trails through the forest. The one-mile Ridding Wood Trail is best suited to families with small children, pushchairs or wheelchairs, while the 1½-mile Millwood Trail makes for a good introduction to the forest.

Ridding Wood Trail
Grade: easy, surfaced trail
Distance: 1 mile; 45 mins
Trailhead: visitor centre
The shortest and easiest trail for little children and buggies. It takes in a beautiful oak woodland and many of the sculptures.

Machells Coppice Trail
Grade: strenuous
Distance: 1½ miles; 1 hr
Trailhead: Machells Coppice car park
A short walk in the far west of the park with views over Coniston Water.

Millwood Trail
Grade: moderate
Distance: 1½ miles; 1 hr
Trailhead: visitor centre
An excellent introduction to the forest, passing under the Go Ape course amid some of the oldest trees in the forest (many over 100 years old).

Bogle Crag Trail
Grade: moderate
Distance: 3 miles; 2 hrs
Trailhead: Bogle Crag car park
Away from the park's main area, this moderate trail highlights some of the artworks, including Anthony Goldsworthy's *Taking A Wall for a Walk*, one of the best-loved works.

Carron Crag Trail
Grade: strenuous
Distance: 3 miles; 2 hrs
Trailhead: visitor centre
A trail to the highest point in the forest (314 m) and an ideal place for a picnic with panoramic views. This trail takes in many of the sculptures in the forest.

Grizedale Tarn Trail
Grade: moderate
Distance: 3½ miles; 2 hrs
Trailhead: visitor centre
This trail takes in the only natural tarn (small lake) in the forest.

High Bowkerstead Trail
Grade: strenuous
Distance: 4 miles; 2 hrs plus
Trailhead: Blind Lane car park
Another off-centre trail, accessed from one of the smaller car parks, this more demanding trail involves a steep climb but the reward is a spectacular vista from the top.

Silurian Way
Grade: strenuous
Distance: 10 miles; 5 hrs
Trailhead: visitor centre
The grand tour of the area, which highlights many of the artworks, ancient trees and outstanding viewpoints.

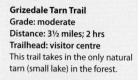

Off the beaten track Grizedale Forest Park

Once there, head for the new £6 million **visitor centre**, which opened in the autumn of 2009. The centre has useful maps and guides to the trails, details of the latest installations on the sculpture trail and news about special events in the park. With an eye on future school projects, you might like to pick up a copy of the Forestry Commission booklet, *An Easy Guide to Forest Trees and their Uses* – great for natural sciences lessons.

Ride a horse
On the site is the **Grizedale Riding Centre** (age 6 and over, from £22/hr easy ride for novices, £43/ 3-hr advanced ride for experienced riders). They offer a half-day riding experience through the Grizedale Forest Park with a packed lunch for £70 a person. Advance bookings only.

Pitch your tent
There's no accommodation on site at Grizedale but you can keep that fresh-air approach to the great outdoors by bedding down at **Bowkerstead Farm** (LA12 8LL, T01229-860208, grizedale-camping. co.uk, from £6 adult, £2.50 child/pitch). The site is located just south of Grizedale in the village of Satterthwaite. It's a rather basic site with no

electricity hook-up, but a large pitching field and a shower block make it popular in summer. The addition of some new camping pods (from £25 night), wooden structures with insulated walls, adds a little more privacy and shelter when the weather turns ugly.

Sleep in a comfy bed
The nearest accommodation with a bed for tired hikers and bikers is the **Grizedale Lodge** (LA22 0QL, T01539-436532, grizedale-lodge.com, from £95/room B&B). It's actually a cut-above a B&B, with eight comfy, if slightly frilly, rooms, all named after trees in the forest. If you're setting out on a long walk, you may be tempted by the house-special breakfast: a bowl of porridge (laced with whisky for the grown-ups).

Also close by is **Pepper House** (LA12 8LS, T01229-860206, pepper-house.co.uk, from £70/ room B&B), a small but friendly local B&B, which is very popular with walkers.

Grab a bite
The new **Café in the Forest** (T01229-860455, year round daily 0930-1700), near Grizedale Visitor Centre, is good for a light bite. Managed in association with Kendal's excellent Brewery Arts Centre (see page 74), it offers snacks, coffees and main meals (£6-8), plus some kids' options.

Just south of Grizedale, in the rustic village of Satterthwaite, the atmospheric **Eagles Head** (T01229-860237) serves bar food (1200-1430 and 1900-2030), with mains around £10; it also has a little beer garden.

Go Ape

Grizedale Forest, nr Hawkshead; Whinlatter Forest, nr Keswick, T0845-643 9215, goape.co.uk. Mar-Oct daily 0900-1700, plus weekends in Nov and Feb half term. From £30 gorilla (18+), £20 baboon (10-17).

Not one, but two opportunities to monkey about on rope ladders, platforms and zip slides in the treetops of the Lake District's forests, as both Grizedale and Whinlatter boast Go Ape courses. Note: each participant is fitted with a harness and given safety instruction before starting the two-hour high-wire course, but the instructor does not accompany participants around the course. There's a minimum age of 10 years, a minimum height restriction of 1.4 m, and anyone under 18 years of age must be supervised by a participating adult. Book ahead.

Check out the wildlife in the Grizedale Forest Park.

Bike the forest

Bike it

Grizedale Mountain Bikes
Grizedale Forest,
T01229-860369,
grizedalemountainbikes.co.uk.
Year round daily 0900-1700, bike
£22/day, child's bike £15/day,
tag-a-long or trailer £10/day.
This bike hire and repair shop,
located near the visitor centre,
is the place for all things on
two wheels in the forest. The
knowledgeable staff will advise
on the best way-marked routes
to take for an easy day visit, plus
other forest roads and public
bridleways if you want a longer
ride. They will, no doubt, remind
you to wear a helmet when
tackling the trails.

There are five way-marked and colour-coded (for difficulty) mountain biking trails through the forest, ranging in length from two miles to 14 miles. The one most suitable for families with older children is the Hawkshead Moor Trail. The North Face Trail is a demanding route designed for serious mountain bikers used to negotiating difficult terrain.

Goosey Foot Tarn Trail
Grade: forest road
Distance: 2 miles; 30 mins
Trailhead: Moor Top
This is the shortest trail, and suitable for less experienced riders. The route takes in Goosey Foot and Juniper tarns but with some hills involved.

Grizedale Tarn Trail
Grade: forest road
Distance: 6 miles; 1½ hrs
Trailhead: Bogle Crag car park
This moderate trail meanders through the forest with woodland views of the eerie Bogle Crag.

Moor Top Trail
Grade: forest road and part public road
Distance: 7 miles; 1½ hrs
Trailhead: visitor centre
A journey though woodland on the lower slopes of the valley, this is a great route for spotting birds, especially early or late in the day.

North Face Mountain Bike Trail
Grade: off road
Distance: 10 miles; 2½ hrs
Trailhead: the visitor centre
This trail requires a high level of skill and fitness. It is based on a single track through the forest and includes lots of adrenaline-pumping sections.

Hawkshead Moor Trail
Grade: forest road
Distance: 10½ miles; 2½ hrs
Trailhead: visitor centre
This trail on the western side of the park affords great views out west to Coniston Old Man, Langdale fells and Helvellyn beyond.

Silurian Way
Grade: forest road and part public road
Distance: 14 miles; 3½ hrs
Trailhead: visitor centre
A moderate but hilly trail covering both sides of the Grizedale valley, it takes in many of the artworks on the sculpture trail.

Looking up Grizedale towards Nethermost Pike.

Out & about Central Lakes

Boat trips
Coniston Launch
Coniston, T01768-775753, conistonlaunch.co.uk. Year round but weekends only Nov-mid-Mar from £7.90 adult, £3.95 child, £20 family.
This follows the route: Coniston Jetty–Torver–Water Park–Lake Bank–Sunny Bank–Brantwood. There is also a Swallows & Amazons Cruise (age 6 and over, 1 hr 50 mins, Mar–Oct, £10.50 adult, £5.50 child) exploring the places that inspired Arthur Ransome's classic children's books. Discounted combination tickets with entry to Brantwood (see page 54).

Keswick Launch
Keswick, T01768-772263, keswick-launch.co.uk. Year round £8.80 adult, £4.40 child, £21 family.
This follows the route: Keswick–Ashness Gate–Lodore–High/Low Brandelhow–Hawes End (for Catbells, see page 48)–Nichol End. There's also a one-hour cruise around Derwentwater.

Steam yacht Gondola
Coniston Pier, T01539-463831, nationaltrust.org.uk/gondola. Apr-Nov round-trip (45 mins) £8 adult, £4 child, £20 family.
This takes the route: Coniston–Brantwood–Monk Coniston. There's also a 90-minute Explorer Cruise (Mon and Thu) along the length of the lake. See page opposite.

❷ The tourist information centre in Bowness-on-Windermere has a little side room off the office with seats and a rolling DVD programme of information films about the Lakes. It offers a rare moment of peace in the high-season scramble.

Windermere Lake Cruises
Bowness-on-Windermere, T01539-443360, windermere-lakecruises.co.uk. Year round, from £8.90 adult, £5 child.
These cruises go Bowness–Ambleside and Bowness–Lakeside. The Freedom of the Lake day pass allows use of all four colour-coded cruises for a 24-hour period from any pier around the lake: £16 adult, £8 child (5-15; under-5s free), £44 family; ask about Freedom Friday Tickets with the above rate discounted to £12.80, £6.40 and £35. Also check out combined tickets, which work out cheaper: combined boat and train fares

from £13.50 adult, £7.20 child, £37 family; combined boat and Aquarium of the Lakes (see page 54) from £15.95 adult, £9.20 child, £47.50 family.

Bushcraft
Woodsmoke
Cockermouth, T01900-821733, woodsmoke.uk.com. Woodlander course £425 person (14-17).
Woodsmoke offers a six-day expedition-style survival course for teenagers near Ambleside.

Canoeing
Windermere Canoe
Bowness-on-Windermere, T015394-44451, windermerecanoekayak.com. Closed Wed mid-Feb-Jan. Kayak and canoe hire from £30/day, £20/half-day; tuition from £28/hr.
Canoes and kayaks for hire, with safety and technique briefing. For an action-packed day on and off the water you can also arrange bike/canoe combos.

Take a cruise on Coniston Water.

Cruise the lake

Steam yacht *Gondola*, Coniston.

Cruising the lakes is one of the quintessential Cumbrian experiences and the steam yacht *Gondola* is the ultimate way to explore Coniston. This grand old dame offers no ordinary lake cruise, for the 45-minute ride (with up to seven departures per day in high season) is a chance to revel in living history.

The cruise combines the experience of travelling in opulent Victorian surroundings with stunning views of Coniston's west and east shores as you chug along at a steady 12 mph. Parents will love sinking into the comfy seats of the cushion-strewn saloon as the *Gondola* pulls gently out from the pier, but kids will probably make a beeline for the deck to explore the hidden nooks and crannies and take a look over the engine room.

On a sunny day, nothing beats sitting out on deck, soaking up the views across to the Old Man of Coniston to the north and Peel Island to the south and listening to the purr of the engine. Friendly staff are happy to provide the low-down on the engine, a two-cylinder, V-shaped affair with a water capacity of 200 gallons. You can also ask staff for a copy of the colour brochure *Steam Yacht Gondola*, produced by the National Trust.

According to Jo Haughton, Marketing Assistant for the National Trust, who promotes the steamer:

"*Gondola* is a completely unique Cumbrian experience. But it's also a labour of love, a consuming passion. It's not just a boat, it's a living, breathing entity. The Trust sees the *Gondola* as iconic. She's a flagship for the Trust and for the area as a whole."

Venerable history
Some major anniversaries of the service fall in 2010: it is 150 years since the original *Gondola* launched on Coniston and 30 years of the current *Gondola* operating on the lake. The current vessel is an inch-by-inch replica of the original *Gondola*, comprising a first-class saloon with red, crushed-velvet sofas, and leather seating, styled on the Victorian train system, in the third-class saloon.

The 150th anniversary of tourism to the area also falls in 2010. Sir James Ramsden, a director of the Furness Railway Company, saw the potential in using the local railway line from Fleetwood to Barrow-in-Furness to bring tourists to the Lake District and propel Coniston to the fore as a tourist destination.

Ramsden commissioned the *Gondola* to complement the railway. It first took to the water on 24 June 1860 and stopped sailing in 1936. In the 1970s, it was salvaged from the bottom of the lake by the National Trust and used as the basis for construction of the current vessel, which launched in 1980. The boat has carried over 650,000 passengers around Coniston since the upholstery in the first-class saloon was refurbished in 1990.

Until 2007 the boat was steam-driven by burning coal, hence a true steamer. Since 2008 it has used sustainable wood-chip logs, a more environmentally friendly fuel, reducing its carbon footprint by around 90%. Operating costs currently stand at £180,000 per year.

The 45-minute circuit of the lake includes two scheduled stops at Brantwood and Monk Coniston, so you can combine a trip on the *Gondola* with a visit to Brantwood, John Ruskin's home (buy discount vouchers on board), or to Tarn Hows and the Monk Coniston Estate, where the Trust has recently completed a £900,000 Heritage Lottery Funded Project to restore key features of the estate.

Anniversary celebrations
The *Gondola*'s anniversary will be marked by a series of events. The crew will wear Victorian costumes and there will be a dressing-up box on board for passengers. The Trust is also planning to run more Gondola Explorer cruises (£15 adult, £7.50 child, £39 family), an extended cruise along the full length of the lake with a commentary from the crew. Take a picnic.

Call ahead for details of forthcoming events, promotions and special excursions.

Essential
information

Coniston Pier, LA21 8AN, T01539-441288, nationaltrust.org.uk/gondola. Apr–Nov daily depending on weather conditions £8 adult, £4 child, £20 family (under-5s free).

Out & about Central Lakes

Climbing
Keswick Climbing Wall
Keswick, T01768-772000, keswickclimbingwall.co.uk. Year-round £12.50 group lesson (age 6 and over), including equipment.
A challenging climbing wall and outdoor activity centre with lessons available for all ages, plus multi-activity days.

Lakeland Climbing Centre
Nr Kendal, LA9 6HN, T01539-721766, kendalwall.co.uk. May-Aug Tue-Sun from 1000. Taster sessions £12 adult, £10 child (8 years and over), Geckos sessions (age 6-10) £10.
A wide range of indoor and outdoor climbing courses for all ages and abilities, including children as young as six at the junior club on Saturdays.

Via Ferrata & Zip
Honister Slate Mine (see page 55). From £35 adult, £25 child (10-15), £115 family.
Follow in the footsteps of Julia Bradbury on BBC's *Countryfile* and scale the sheer rock face of the old miners' route using fixed cables then sail down on the zip wire. Not one for the faint-hearted.

Cycling
Country Lanes
Windermere train station, T01539-444544, countrylaneslakedistrict.co.uk. Easter-Nov from £19 day mountain bike, £10 day child's bike (24-in wheel), tag-a-long or trailer, £45/family fun ticket.

Offers bike hire, cycle tour packages, and boat trips combined with bike hire. You can take a cruiser to Lakeside at the southern tip of Windermere, where two-hour cycle routes link the villages of Finsthwaite and Newby Bridge, or follow the River Leven (and steam train line) to Haverthwaite.

Cycling routes around Coniston
The wooded eastern shore of Coniston Water is very scenic and offers one of the easiest stretches of on-road cycling in Cumbria, a perfect excursion for family bike rides. In fact, the area around Coniston is a stand-out location for cyclists in the Central Lakes in general, with routes of varying difficulty.

The three routes listed here make use of parts of the National Cycle Network (NCN) Regional Route 37, running between Ambleside and Ulverston; more details from sustrans.org.uk. Before you set out, pick up a copy of the leaflet *Cycling from Coniston in the Lake District National Park* for maps and further route guidance; more details from cyclingcumbria.co.uk.

You can hire bikes from **Gill Cycles** (Ulverston, T01229-581116, gillcycles.co.uk) or **Grizedale Mountain Bikes** (T01229-860369, grizedalemountainbikes.co.uk).

The three main routes are:

Tarn Hows
Distance: 9 miles
Start: pay-and-display car park next to Coniston's tourist information office
Grade: short challenge
Stop at: Yew Tree Farm tearoom (see page 70)
Suitable for: teenagers and more experienced riders

Little Langdale
Distance: 9½ miles
Start: pay-and-display car park next to Coniston's tourist information office
Grade: short challenge
Stop at: Yew Tree Farm tearoom (see page 70)
Suitable for: teenagers and mountain bikers

Coniston Water and Lowick Bridge
Distance: 17½ miles
Start: pay-and-display car park next to Coniston's tourist information office
Grade: moderate–easy
Stop at: Bluebird Café at Coniston Boating Centre (see page 72)
Suitable for: families and general riders

Fishing
Hawkshead Trout Farm
Hawkshead, LA22 0QF, T01539-436541, hawksheadtrout.com. Year round daily 0900-1800. £26 adult/4 fish, £12 child/2 fish.
Offers brown and rainbow trout fishing in summer, and winter

Take the family on a climb up Catbells

Feeling the need to coax the family up at least one Lakeland peak during your stay? Good for you, Dad. And here's your answer: Catbells, the 'shelter of the wild cat'. Or, in high summer, the shelter of the truculent teenager.

Alfred Wainwright, the authority on walking in the Lakes, wrote: "Catbells is one of the great favourites, a family fell where grandmothers and infants can climb the heights together."

The well-trodden Catbells trail is hugely popular with a bulging ant trail weaving its way up the mountain at regular intervals during summer. But don't be fooled. Though well-trodden and relatively easy to access, it does have some bite. Craggy flanks rub shoulders with grassy slopes and the high-level views of Borrowdale and Derwentwater are intoxicating.

The best way to access the trailhead at Hawse End is by boat from Keswick Pier. From here, it's a 1½ mile ascent to the summit at 451m; the first tantalizing view of the climb ahead is visible from a clearing in the trees close to the landing stage. If the steep lower slope from the cattle grid looks too daunting, head left to the Woodford's Path, a series of zigzags, which are a gentler, more enjoyable start to the ascent. The final leg to the summit comprises three depressions, the first of which offers some shelter if the weather turns.

Coming down, it's an easy, two-mile descent to Grange in Borrowdale via Hause Gate, followed by a walk through the valley to Lodore landing stage, where you can take a launch back to Keswick. Aside from the zigzags below Hause Gate, the descent is set at an easy gradient, making for a gentle stroll down.

Of course, serious baggers of the 214 Wainwrights would baulk at such a mainstream trail, but let them scoff. If your family makes it up just one peak in the Lake District National Park, then make it Catbells.

More information from:
golakes.co.uk/adventure-capital/walking-lake-district.aspx
wainwright.org.uk/links/index.html
juliabradbury.com/walks.html

fishing for pike on Esthwaite Water. It has a zoned-off area for children and can supply tackle as part of the day package.

Multi activities
Joint Adventures
Coniston, T015394-41526, jointadventures.co.uk. Family adventure activity courses (tailor made) £160/day, children's adventure day (3 activities) £40 child. Abseiling, canoeing, ghyll and gorge scrambling, kayaking, orienteering, raft building and rock climbing.

Lakeland Mountain Ventures
Kendal, T01539-741318, lakelandmountainventures.co.uk. From £75/day (2-3 activities for 4 or more people), £45/day (1 activity). Abseiling, canoeing, ghyll and gorge scrambling, mountain biking, ridge walking, rock climbing and wild camping.

Newlands Adventure Centre
Stair, nr Keswick, T01768-778463, activity-centre.com. Courses from £20 person/day – call ahead for promotions. Mountain biking, ghyll and gorge scrambling, climbing and abseiling, canoeing and kayaking, archery and orienteering.

River Deep Mountain High
Low Wood, T01539-531116, riverdeepmountainhigh.co.uk. Full day (2 activities) £77 adult, £55 child (16 and under); half-day £44 person, £33 child (8 and under). Bike hire not included.

Abseiling, archery, canoeing, ghyll scrambling, kayaking, mountain biking, raft building, rock climbing and sailing.

Paragliding
Tandem Paragliding
Keswick, T01768-771442, keswickparagliding.com. From £90 tandem flights.
Thirty-minute tandem flights over beautiful Lakeland scenery.

Sailing
Coniston Boating Centre
Coniston, LA21 8EW, T01539-441366, lake-district.gov.uk. From £35/ wayfarers, £18/toppers (minimum 2 hrs).
Plot a course for Wild Cat Island of *Swallows and Amazons* fame. If you need sailing lessons, this RYA centre offers tuition in toppers and other easy-to-sail dinghies. Electric motor boats, rowing boats and Canadian canoes are also available to hire.

Derwentwater Marina
Portinscale, T01768-772912, derwentwatermarina.co.uk. From £160 RYA 2-day sailing course, hourly rental charges: £17/pico, £10/canoe.
A wide range of sailing courses, including RYA Youth Stages.

Water sports
Lakes Leisure Windermere
Windermere, T015394-47183, lakesleisure.org.uk. From £24 adult, £19 child for introductory courses.
A range of courses and multi-activity days with a choice

of canoeing, sailing and windsurfing.

Low Wood Watersports
Windermere, T015394-39441, elh. co.uk. Sailing tuition £80/2 hrs, wayfarer dinghy hire £35/2 hrs. Sailing, canoeing tuition and rental, plus rowing boats, motor boats and water skiing.

Platty+
Lodore Boat Landing, Derwentwater, CA12 5UX, T01768-776572, plattyplus.co.uk. From £46/2 hrs sailing tuition, £23/hr laser dinghy hire; £210/2 hrs Viking long ship (10 people).
RYA courses, dinghy and canoe hire, plus a chance to sail in a replica Viking long ship or paddle a dragon boat.

Cycle or walk around Keswick

Keswick is a great base for some gentle exercise for all ages. The pick of the local operators are **Keswick Mountain Bikes** (T01768-775202, keswickbikes.co.uk) and **Keswick Climbing Wall** (T01768-772000, keswickclimbingwall.co.uk). More from cyclingcumbria.co.uk.

The Miles without Stiles programme covers 39 'road tested' routes through the national park, ideal for those in wheelchairs, with buggies or who find walking a challenge. For selected walks in the Keswick area, see lakedistrict.gov.uk/index/visiting/outdoors/mileswithoutstiles.htm.

For guided walks, contact **Keswick Rambles** (T01768-771302, keswickrambles.org.uk) and **Pace the Peaks** (T01768-774824, pacethepeaks.co.uk). More from keswick.org/walks.asp. Before you set out, get kitted out for action at **George Fisher** (T01768-772178, georgefisheronline.co.uk), Keswick's favourite outdoor shop. If the bad weather sets in, the top-floor café, Abraham's Tearoom, is a cosy place to pore over maps and dream of what might have been.

Don't miss the Wordsworth Trail

Dove Cottage, Grasmere.

William Wordsworth is without doubt Cumbria's most celebrated literary figure and 2010 marks 240 years since his birth and 160 years since his death, both in the month of April.

If you have teenage children struggling with Wordsworth at school, visiting a few places associated with the great poet can do wonders for helping them 'get' his poetry and the Romantic Movement in general. Even young children can delight in the rhymes and rhythms of the perennial-favourite *Daffodils* and soon be precociously chanting:

' I wandered lonely as a cloud
That floats on high o'er vales and hills'.

The most famous Wordsworth landmarks are in the Central Lakes. They are always very busy, but try to look beyond the crowds, the shutterbugs and the heaving coach and car parks. Following the Wordsworth trail is all about sharing Wordsworth's deep love of the Lakes and celebrating their raw beauty, an appreciation which he saw as a universal entitlement. Wordsworth himself called the landscape, 'A sort of national property, in which every man has a right and interest who has an eye to perceive and a heart to enjoy'.

For more on following the Wordsworth trail in Cumbria, see visitcumbria.com/wilword.htm.

Cockermouth

The Wordsworth House, Wordsworth's early childhood home in **Cockermouth**, is the starting point for the Wordsworth Trail and the most child-friendly of the attractions along the Wordsworth Trail. The property has a superb living-history feel with staff in period costume running the house as if it is still the 18th century. Unusually for a stately home, it's very hands on, so kids will love dressing up, picking flowers in the garden and watching the maids prepare fresh bread in the kitchen. It's an educational visit but also great fun. For more details, see page 157.

Grasmere

The main point of interest for visitors is Grasmere, which Wordsworth once described as 'the fairest place on earth'. And the key attraction is **Dove Cottage**, the cramped, whitewashed former coaching inn where the Wordsworth family lived from 1799 to 1808. William wrote much of his best poetry here, and his sister Dorothy kept her famous diary, later published as the *Grasmere Journal*, while living in the cottage with William, his wife Mary Hutchinson and, later, their three eldest children, John born in 1803, Dora in 1804 and Thomas in 1806.

Dove Cottage is so popular with overseas visitors that it is regularly swamped. Entry is therefore controlled by a timed ticket for a 20-minute guided tour with one of the curators, which can make a visit rather crowded and regimented for children. While the official tour focuses on daily life at the cottage, a visit to the cottage garden and the orchard that the family loved may be more rewarding. The important thing for children is to soak up the atmosphere.

The charitable Wordsworth Trust (T01539-463520, wordsworth.org.uk) turned Dove Cottage into a museum in 1981. Together with the Wordsworth Library, it houses one of the greatest collections of manuscripts, books and paintings

Anniversary

In 2010 Cumbria Tourism (golakes.co.uk) is promoting a programme of events to mark Wordsworth's contribution to British literature. Call ahead for details and expect even bigger than usual crowds at locations associated with Wordsworth.

❸ Wordsworth and Samuel Taylor Coleridge published *The Lyrical Ballads* together in 1798. Two years later they discovered Dove Cottage on a walking tour of Cumbria. Wordsworth returned shortly after to make it his home and live the poet's life of which he had dreamed.

relating to British Romanticism. School age children with GCSEs looming may enjoy one of the regular poetry evenings staged by the Trust, both on site and in the Jerwood Centre, just down the road from Dove Cottage. Admission is free but booking is recommended.

Another atmospheric spot is the **Wordsworth family grave** in St Oswald's churchyard in the heart of the village of Grasmere. Lying in the shade of a yew tree, one of eight planted by the poet in the churchyard, the graves of William, Mary and Dorothy, plus several of the children, provide a relatively peaceful counterpoint to the brouhaha down the road. For a family stroll, the **Wordsworth Daffodil Garden** is a gentle trail along the fringe of the graveyard. The path, alive with wild flowers in spring, is managed by the Friends of Grasmere to raise funds to preserve the churchyard.

Ambleside

Three miles along the A591 towards Ambleside from Dove Cottage, the turn-off to **Rydal Mount** leads to a stately house that was the Wordsworth family home for 37 years from 1813 to 1850. Today the house belongs to the descendants of the poet and retains a lived-in family ambience, offering a more personal experience than a visit to Dove Cottage. The house itself appeals more to adults with its numerous portraits, personal possessions and first

Wordsworth House, Cockermouth.

editions of the poet's work. But for children, it's Rydal Mount's four-acre garden, in which William loved to potter, that will hold the most interest. The garden, with views across to Rydal Water, remains much as he designed it, with rare shrubs, rock pools and an ancient mound. It's a great spot to run off some energy, explore hidden nooks and crannies, and connect to Wordsworth's verse. Spring, in particular, brings a spectacular display of colour, with daffodils, bluebells and rhododendrons. In fact, Wordsworth was reported to joke that, if he hadn't been a poet, he would have wanted to be a gardener.

Ask at the ticket office for the leaflet detailing a walk around the garden, highlighting 26 plants and trees of special interest. Children can follow the trail like a treasure hunt, ticking off their finds as they explore.

Hawkshead
The last site on the trail is on the edge of the village of Hawkshead, where the **Hawkshead Grammar School** was a cornerstone of academic discipline for young William and his older brother John. William arrived at the school in 1778 and left in 1787 to continue his education at Cambridge.

The dusty schoolroom with its chalk and slates is a far cry from the white boards and computer terminals of today's classrooms. Children will be amazed to see how previous generations went about their learning and no doubt relieved that Latin, Greek and trigonometry are no longer the cornerstones of the curriculum that they were in Wordsworth's time. Only the forbidding headmaster's office has survived the test of time to remind them of their own school.

After your visit, check out the distinctive sundial on the main façade of the schoolhouse and take a stroll around the grounds of St Michael's Church next door. William often did while thinking up excuses for why he hadn't done his homework.

The Wordsworth family grave, Grasmere.

Out & about Central Lakes

Aquarium of the Lakes

Lakeside, LA12 8AS, T01539-530153, aquariumofthelakes.co.uk.
Year round daily 0900-1800, winter 1700, £8.95 adult, £5.95 child (3-15), £26.95 family.

One mile northeast of Newby Bridge, off the A590, the Aquarium of the Lakes contains all sorts of aquatic species – from piranhas to Asian otters. Try to time your visit to coincide with the daily feeding times (1030 and 1500) for the best of the action.

But the exotic species are all upstaged by the Cumbrian critters, thanks to some clever exhibits. Best of all is a walk-through tunnel where you can watch diving ducks, their bodies cloaked in silvery sheens of trapped air, swimming through shoals of carp. Elsewhere you'll see brown trout leaping through tiered aquariums, and come nose-to-nose with rays and sharks in the Morecambe Bay pool. There's also an exhibition on the Lake District's very own mystery monster, Bownessie. And if your kids need a high-tech fix, steer them towards the Virtual Dive Bell, where they can embark on an interactive adventure with sharks, hippos and crocodiles. Younger children can pick up a quiz sheet at reception and follow Oscar the Otter's trail around the exhibition.

The aquarium is very much a one-stop shop for a big day out. For a quick lunch on site, Oscars Bistro, next to the landing stage at the southern terminus for the Windermere Lake Cruises, is a bit of a tourist trap but offers family-friendly facilities, such as high chairs, baby food-warming, kids' meals (around £3), as well as mains for around £5, coffee and cakes.

Brantwood

Coniston, LA21 8AD, T01539-441396, brantwood.org.uk. Mid-Mar to mid-Nov daily 1100-1730, low season 1100-1630, £6.30 adult, £1.35 child, £13.15 family, £4.50 gardens only.

The erstwhile home of the Victorian thinker and polymath John Ruskin is a testament to his aesthetic tastes in architecture, garden design and collecting. It hosts regular exhibitions, while eight individual gardens making up the 25-acre wooded estate combine unique features with colourful displays and panoramic views of Coniston. During school holidays, a range of activities suitable for children aged five to 10 years (£5 child) takes place in the house and gardens, including a garden trail designed specifically for kids that lets them run free through the grounds. There is also a café and gift shop.

The Brantwood jetty offers access to the steam yacht *Gondola* (see page 45) and the Coniston Launch (see page 44) for discounted combination tickets.

If you are coming by car, Brantwood is about three miles southeast of Coniston on the eastern side of Coniston Water. Follow the B5285 then the brown signs.

Brantwood Jetty, Cockermouth.

Hill Top

Nr Sawrey, LA22 0LE, T01539-436269, nationaltrust.org.uk/beatrixpotter. House Mar-Oct Sat-Thu 1030-1630, Feb and Nov Sat-Thu 1100-1530, garden daily summer 1030-1700, winter 1100-1600, £6.20 adult, £3.10 child (under-5s free), £15.50 family with timed admission tickets (garden free when house closed).

Beatrix Potter's famous cottage, situated in a rural Lakeland hamlet, two miles south of Hawkshead on the B5285, is a site of pilgrimage. Indeed, it's so popular with Japanese visitors that a replica of Hill Top has been built at Daito Bunka University in Tokyo.

Look past the crowds, however, and the charms of rural life in an idyllic location are manifest. Potter bought the farmhouse in November 1905 for £2085, using the profits from her first published books, including *The Tale of Peter Rabbit*. The cottage has barely changed since her death in 1943, when she left it and several other properties to the National Trust. If the queue to get in is too off-putting, the garden and vegetable patch are a delightful, nature-filled place where children can play, just as Peter Rabbit did.

A note of caution: parking is limited, so expect queues.

Honister Slate Mine

Honister Pass, nr Keswick, CA12 5XN, T01768-777230, honister-slate-mine. co.uk. Year round daily 0900-1700. Mine tours £9.75 adult, £4.75 child, £27 family.

The last working slate mine in England, on the B5289 10 miles northwest of Keswick, Honister is a great wet-weather bolthole. A range of guided tours departing from the visitor centre lead deep underground, where the slate is still mined. The Kimberley tour is suitable for all ages, while The Edge tour has a minimum height of 1.3 m. Best of all for adrenaline-pumping thrills is England's first Via Ferrata ('iron way', – an adventure climbing system based on the miners' way of travelling over the cliff face). In 2009 an exciting new zip wire was added, soaring 120 m over the valley floor. See also page 46.

Lakeside & Haverthwaite Railway

Lakeside, LA12 8AL, T01539-531594, lakesiderailway.co.uk. Apr-Oct daily, £5.90 adult return, £2.95 child, £16 family.

This 19th-century standard-gauge railway forms part of the popular Lakeside complex, along with the Aquarium of the Lakes (see above). It was once the iron horse that carried Cumbria's industrial materials, but now it's simply one of the most popular vintage steam railways in northern Britain. The lost-in-time carriages huff and

Keswick's famous writers

Keswick has strong associations with many 19th- and early 20th-century writers, most famously, as far as children are concerned, with Beatrix Potter (1866-1943), who spent many summers at Lingholm and Fawe Park, two large estates on the shores of Derwentwater. Scenes of life around the lake inspired some of her stories: *The Tale of Squirrel Nutkin* is based on Derwentwater, with Owl Island being St Herbert's Island, and Mrs Tiggy-Winkle's home was inspired by Catbells. See also Hill Top, opposite.

Meanwhile, Arthur Ransome (1884-1967) based the children's look-out point in *Swallows and Amazons* on Friar's Crag, overlooking Derwentwater near Keswick. It is one of several local sites said to have inspired the nautical adventures of the Walker and Blackett children.

The Keswick area also inspired the Lakeland poets, whose poems drew the first tourists to visit the area. William Wordsworth (1770-1850) and his sister Dorothy stayed at Old Windebrowe near Keswick for several months, while Robert Southey (1774-1843), Poet Laureate in 1813, lived at Greta Hall and is buried at Crosthwaite Church. Wordswoth's friend and collaborator Samuel Taylor Coleridge (1772-1834), best known for *The Rime of the Ancient Mariner*, also lived at Greta Hall, but deserted his family for a life of opium addiction in London, leaving Robert Southey to support them.

puff their way along tracks from Lakeside to Haverthwaite via Newby Bridge and back, with journeys timed to coincide with the arrivals and departures of Windermere Lake Cruises.

Look out for off-season special journeys, including the Santa Family Outing and Days Out with Thomas the Tank Engine during half term.

You can combine a visit to the Aquarium with a ride on one of the steam trains. Return fares, plus aquarium entry, cost £11.95 adult, £6.60 child and £35.50 family. Buy tickets from the kiosks by the pay-and-display car park.

You can also combine the train ride with a boat trip on Windermere (see Windermere Lake Cruises, page 44), a good opportunity to leave the car behind and complete a full circuit of the lake by public transport. Fares from £18.70 adult, £9.35 child, £52 family.

Mirehouse

Keswick, CA12 4QE, T017687-72287, mirehouse.com. Apr-Oct: gardens daily 1000-1700, house Sun and Wed plus Fri in Aug, house and grounds £6.50 adult, £3 child, £18 family.
The 17th-century manor at Mirehouse, on the A591 three miles northwest of Keswick, has quiz trails for children and a tearoom serving local fare such as Cumberland sausage and gingerbread. The only problem is how to lure kids inside

when they would far rather be out playing in the grounds. Sweeping down to the shores of Bassenthwaite, the estate's gardens include four woodland playgrounds, including a Forest Hazard Course for 12-16-year-olds, plus a heather maze and nature trail.

World of Beatrix Potter

Bowness-on-Windermere, T01539-488444, hop-skip-jump.com. Summer 1000-1730, winter to 1630, £6.75 adult, £3.50 child.
Konichiwa. And welcome to little Tokyo-on-Windermere, where coach parties gather en masse to witness Peter Rabbit, Mrs Tiggy-Winkle, Jemima Puddle-Duck et al brought to life in Lake District

Beatrix Potter's garden.

Beatrix Potter's house.

scenes that evoke all 23 of Potter's tales. If the scrum to be served at the Beatrix Potter gift shop gets too much, there's a little tearoom, serving Tabitha Twitchit's High Tea (£5.95) for adults and Cotton Tail's Toast Soldiers (£1.95) for kids. A welcome addition is the new Peter Rabbit Garden with nature trails and puzzles for kids. It's a good escape from the throngs, and brings the stories to life with its gooseberry bushes, fruit trees and rows of organic vegetables. There is also a programme of special events, including Peter Rabbit tea parties, staged year round. So all together now: 'Kawaii' – how cute!

❷ The World of Beatrix Potter runs a children's clothes shop on Crag Brow, but there's more of interest next door in The Toy Chest.

Rain check

Arts & crafts
• **Colourpots Café**, Bowness-on-Windermere, T01539-448877, colourpots.co.uk. Pots from £1.50 plus £3 studio fees.
• **Pots of Love**, Kendal, T01539-724437, lovepots.co.uk. Pots plus glazing from £6.50 and ready to collect in three days.

Arts venues
• **Brewery Arts Centre**, Kendal, T01539-725133, breweryarts.co.uk. A sprawling arts centre with three cinemas, a theatre and music venue. It hosts parent and baby and tots 'n' toddlers film screenings on Thursdays (both £4.50), plus Europe's biggest festival of mountain cultures, the Kendal Mountain Festival (mountainfest. co.uk) each November. See also Posh Nosh (page 74).
• **Theatre by the Lake**, Keswick, T01768-774411, theatrebythelake. com.
Situated at the side of Derwentwater, this arts centre is Cumbria's only year-round theatre. Regular events in the calendar include the Keswick Film Festival in February, a literature festival in March and the Keswick Jazz Festival in May. The café and bar open daily from 0930 until the end of the performance.

Cinemas
• **Alhambra Cinema**, Keswick, T017687-72195, keswick-alhambra. co.uk.
• **Royalty**, Bowness-on-Windermere, T015394-43364.
• **Zeffirellis**, T015394-33845, Ambleside, zeffirellis.com.
See also page 73.

Indoor play & amusements
• **Keswick Climbing Wall**, Keswick, T01768-772000, keswickclimbingwall.co.uk
• **Quayside Kids**, Bowness-on-Windermere, T01539-445354, quaysidekids.co.uk

Indoor swimming pools
• **Keswick Leisure Pool & Fitness Centre**, Keswick, T01768-772760, carlisleleisure.com/keswick
• **Lakes Leisure Kendal**, T01539-729777, lakesleisure.org.uk.

Museums
• **Kendal Museum**, Kendal, T01539-721374, kendalmuseum.org.uk. Includes exhibits in memory of its former curator, Alfred Wainwright (see page 48); free entry for children.
• **Keswick Museum & Art Gallery**, T01768-773263, allerdale.gov.uk/keswick-museum.
• **Museum of Lakeland Life**, Kendal, T01539-722464, lakelandmuseum. org.uk. Includes exhibits relating to Arthur Ransome's *Swallows and Amazons* stories.

Out & about Central Lakes

Beatrix Potter Gallery

Hawkshead, LA22 0NS, T01539-436355, nationaltrust.org.uk/beatrixpotter. Mar-Oct Sat-Thu 1030-1630, Feb and Nov Sat-Thu 1100-1530, £4 adult, £2 child.
The fruits of the National Trust's Beatrix Potter archive are on display in this tiny, low-ceilinged (mind your head!) cottage. Amongst the highlights is a collection of Potter's watercolours and sketchbooks, featuring early sketches of her best-loved characters. Downstairs is given over to a recreation of the former offices of Potter's husband, William Heelis, who worked as a solicitor in Hawkshead during the mid-19th century. There's a free activity sheet for children.

You can buy tickets from the National Trust shop across the street, with discounts for those with a valid ticket for Hill Top (see page 55).

Cars of the Stars

Keswick, CA12 5LS, T01768-773757, carsofthestars.com. Easter-Dec, plus Feb half term, daily from 1000, £5 adult, £3 child (3-15).
Featuring four-wheel icons from the silver screen, this motor museum is home to Chitty Chitty Bang Bang, the Batmobiles, Harry Potter's Ford Anglia, Mr Bean's Mini and, the most recent arrival, Starsky & Hutch's Torino. The owner, Peter Nelson, also owns

the James Bond Museum (see page opposite).

Homes of Football

Ambleside, LA22 0DB, T01539-434440, homesoffootball.co.uk. Year round daily 1000-1700, free.
Fans of football or sports photography, or ideally both, will love this contemporary photographic gallery dedicated to the soccer-worshipping lens of local photographer Stuart Roy Clarke. The images are for sale.

Puzzling Place

Keswick, CA12 5DZ, T01768-775102, puzzlingplace.co.uk. Nov-mid Mar Tue-Sun 1100-1730, mid-Mar to Oct daily 1100-1730, £3.50 adult, £2.75 child, £11 family.
Gadgets, gizmos, holograms and puzzles are de rigueur at this puzzle centre. Check out the Anti-Gravity Room for the best optical illusions.

Ruskin Museum

Coniston, LA21 8DU, T01539-441164, ruskinmuseum.com. Year round daily 1000-1730, £4.50 adult, £2 child.
Packed with local history and artefacts, this village museum focuses on John Ruskin, who is well represented with his writings, sketchbooks and drawings, and the Campbell family, serial breakers of the world water-speed record. A new extension to the museum, due to open in 2011, will house the salvaged Bluebird boat (see Remember the Campbells, page 36).

Sizergh Castle & Gardens

Kendal, LA8 8AE, T015395 60951, nationaltrust.org.uk/main/w-sizerghcastlegarden. Mid-Mar to Oct Sun-Thu noon-1700, £7.50 adult, £3.80 child, £11.30 family.
A National Trust property with medieval origins and many Elizabethan features, Sizergh Castle is crammed with history and set in lovely flower-filled gardens. It is situated off the A590 just south of Kendal and close to Low Sizergh Barn (see page 70). Visit the kitchen herb garden and follow the children's outdoor trail, or join in one of the regular family-friendly events, from autumn sculpture making to spring pancake races. The café and shop also opens Saturday 1100-1600.

Threlkeld Quarry & Mining Museum

Nr Keswick, CA12 4TT, T01768-779747, threlkeldminingmuseum.co.uk. Easter-Oct daily 1000-1700, underground mine tour £5 adult, £2.50 child, museum £3 adult, £1.50 child.
Granite, lead and copper were all mined or quarried in Cumbria and this heritage is explored in underground guided tours and a narrow-gauge industrial railway. The museum has the largest collection of cable excavators in Europe with more than 50 examples.

Trotters World of Animals
Bassenthwaite, CA12 4RD, T01768-776239, trottersworld.com. Year round daily 1000-1730, £7.25 adult, £5.25 child, under-3s free.

This small but popular wildlife park is home to lots of unusual species, such as the Asian fishing cat, Canadian lynx and mandrill – the primate with the bright blue nose and bottom. Kids will love hunting for the Celtic roundhouse in the woods or the native American tepee. There are also flying displays, feeding demonstrations and the chance to handle some of the animals. Facilities also include indoor and outdoor children's play areas, a tearoom and a gift shop.

Visit The Bond Museum

Why? Simple. This independently owned museum, which opened in 2009, is the ideal escape for anyone shaken and stirred by the adventures of Britain's best-loved spy on Her Majesty's Secret Service. The hangar-like building is home to a vast collection of cars from the various films, including Roger Moore's Lotus Esprit Turbo in *For Your Eyes Only* and Pierce Brosnan's Aston Martin Vanquish in *Die Another Day*. In 2010 the museum plans to expand to accommodate vehicles from the latest crop of films starring Daniel Craig.

Where? Keswick, CA12 5NR. Behind the Cumberland Pencil Museum.

How? Year round daily 1000-1700, £6 adult, £4 child, £20 family. Park in the pay-and-display car park, or take the Keswick Launch from locations around Derwentwater to the Keswick pier. From there it's a 15-minute walk through the centre of town.

Contact The Bond Museum, T01768-775007, thebondmuseum.com. See also Cars of the Stars, opposite.

The Bond Museum, Keswick.

Hit or miss?

Cumberland Pencil Museum
Keswick, CA12 5NG, T017687-73626, pencilmuseum.co.uk. Year round daily 0930-1700, £3.25 adult, £1.75 child, £8.25 family (under-5s free).

Is this an opportunity to sharpen your children's creativity or a sketchy attempt at a family attraction? In today's hi-tech world, HB could so easily stand for 'horrendously boring'. In fact, you'll be intrigued as soon as you step inside and learn that graphite was first discovered in nearby Borrowdale Valley in the early 1500s. Then there's the record-breaking 7.6 m-long pencil and a Drawing Zone where kids can graft away with every shade of graphite imaginable.

During school holidays the museum hosts workshops and activities, which are great wet-weather distractions. The Fine Art Gift Shop and Sketchers Coffee Shop, the latter with home-baked cakes, kids' lunch boxes and gluten-free goodies, completes the picture.

Mural, pointing to the Cumberland Pencil Museum, Keswick

❸ The best way to sharpen a pencil is with a sharp pocket knife. Pocket sharpeners blunt quickly and blunt blades will simply break the lead. Coloured leads are more fragile and need extra care.

Let's go to…

Ambleside

You can't get much more central than Ambleside. Situated at the foot of the Kirkstone Pass, at the northern head of Windermere, it's a highly popular base for visitors, especially walkers. The town has excellent facilities, many of the most enticing Lakeland fells are within easy striking distance, and the blockbuster attractions of the Central Lakes are a short drive away, albeit on increasingly crowded roads in summer.

Ambleside was a bustling commercial centre in the Victorian era, with heavy industry its mainstay. Its dark-grey slate buildings are still marked by the industrial age, but tourism is now the breadwinner, with an explosion of outdoors shops doing a roaring trade in fleeces, boots and hiking equipment for the throngs of fell walkers who visit the town each year.

The waters of Lake Windermere lap the southern fringe of Ambleside and offer a host of activities, including fishing, water sports and lake cruises. For details of water-based courses, try **Low Wood Water sports and Activity Centre** (T01539-439441, elh.co.uk/watersports).

Get your bearings
Ambleside is one of the main traffic intersections of the Central Lakes and therefore prone to congestion. From the M6 (junction 36), the A591 leads through Windermere, then Ambleside and on to Keswick, while the A593 leads southwest via Hawkshead and Coniston.

The town is also an important bus interchange, with regular services to Grasmere, Windermere, Coniston and Hawkshead. The main bus station is located in the southwest corner of the town centre, next to a pay-and-display car park sometimes used for a local market. The nearest train station is at Oxenholme, near Kendal.

If you're arriving by boat with **Windermere Lake Cruises** (see page 44), it's a one-mile walk to the centre of town,

Rohan

Ambleside centre at night.

along Lake Road, passing Hayes Garden World on the way. Alternatively, a shuttle-bus service runs to the town centre and costs £1.50 adult, £1 child.

The place to start exploring Ambleside is **The Hub** (LA22 9BS, T01539-432582, tic@ thehubofambleside.com), the tourist information centre-cum-post office in the centre of town. The multi-purpose facility will help book accommodation, advise on local events and sells all sorts of useful essentials from local guides to fishing permits.

Just down the road, it's worth browsing the shelves at **Fred Holdsworth Books** (T01539-434838, fredontheweb.co.uk), a treasure trove of local interest books, maps and guides. This independent bookshop has been around for over 50 years and has the local knowledge to match.

Soak up the history

A stroll around the centre reveals a town rich in history, from the Romans, who constructed a fort, Galava, here in AD 79, to the mills and waterwheels of Ambleside's industrial heyday in the 18th and 19th centuries.

The most famous, and the most photographed, historical site is **Bridge House**, also

Don't miss

Old Courthouse Gallery
T01539-443022, ocg-arts.com
A showcase of contemporary arts and crafts, much of it handmade by local Cumbrian artists. Works include paintings, glassware and ceramics.

Ambleside's smallest attraction. Originally built as an apple store by the Braithwaites of Ambleside Hall in 1723, the tiny building is now owned by the National Trust and houses its shop (Easter-Oct). It clings precariously to the bridge over Stock Beck.

❷ Local artist Alfred Heaton Cooper imported the Alpine-style Log House on Lake Road log by log from Norway with the intention of using it as his art studio. Today, the Log House is a restaurant (T01539-431077) with a decidedly herring-free menu.

On Rydal Road, on the northeast outskirts of town, the **Armitt Museum** (LA22 9BL, T01539-431212, armitt.com, Mon–Sat 1000-1700, £2.50 adult, £1 child, under-5s free) is a museum, gallery

Let's go to... Ambleside

and library that explores the history of Ambleside. Its collection includes watercolours by Beatrix Potter, historic photographs of Ambleside, and paintings by the German artist Kurt Schwitters, who settled in Ambleside after fleeing Nazi persecution. Hands-on children's activities are organized during school holidays.

Back in the centre of town, just south of Market Cross on Church St, is the **Old Stamp House**, where William Wordsworth worked after being appointed the Director of Stamps for Westmorland in 1813. The job may not sound a bundle of laughs, but it helped to fund his move from Dove Cottage (see page 51).

The last stop on the history trail is **St Mary's Church** on the fringe of grassy Rothay Park. It contains a mural painted by the artist Gordon Ranson in 1944, depicting the annual rush-bearing ceremony, a major event in Ambleside's summer calendar when locals parade around town with bundles of rushes and reeds.

Finally, if the kids are grumbling, head into Rothay Park with its green fields, children's play area and riverside footpath to Rothey Holme.

---

❷ St Mary's Church was designed by Sir George Gilbert Scott, who also designed St Pancras Station and the Albert Memorial in Hyde Park.

Browse the shelves

The name to drop around Ambleside is **Lucy's Specialist Grocer** (see page 70) but, while Nigella fans will be licking their spoons with delight, kids may quickly tire of all the foodie one-upmanship. So head across the road to **The Ambleside Toy Shop** (T01539-433780, theamblesidetoyshop. co.uk), a gloriously traditional toy shop with some lovely wooden toys. Also worth a look is **Shinglers** (T01539-433433, shinglers-ambleside.co.uk) for toys, games and art materials.

Ambleside is also a good place to replenish your outdoor gear in one of the many fleece-vending outlets dotted around town. Try these for the latest outdoor wear: **Head to the Hills** (T01539-433826,

Essential websites

amblesideonline.co.uk
golakes.co.uk/places/towns/ambleside.aspx

Old Stamp House, Ambleside.

headtothehills.co.uk); **Gaynor Sports** (T01539-432602, gaynors.co.uk); and **Climber's Shop** (T01539-432297, climbers-shop.com).

Finally, if you're self catering, there's a **Spar** (daily 0800-2200) and **Co-op** (Mon-Sat 0830-2000, Sun 1000-1800).

For more detailed sleeping and eating options, see pages 64-69 and 70-75.

Hike and bike

Ambleside is a walkers' hub, and some of the trails are suitable for families. **Loughrigg Terrace** is one of the best easy-level walks in the area, with superb views over Grasmere and Rydal Water; **Wansfell** is a relatively easy climb with an option to extend the trail to **Troutbeck** or **Townend**. Alternatively, **Jenkin Crag** in Skelghyll Wood was voted one of Britain's most romantic picnic spots.

The fells to the west of Ambleside are a great introduction to off-road cycling for active families with school age kids. The circular, eight-mile tour around **Loughrigg Fell** takes in lakes, woodland and country lanes, while Troutbeck and Ambleside are linked by old bridleways across the southern flanks of Wansfell.

For local bike hire, try **Ghyllside Cycles** (T01539-433592, ghyllside.co.uk) and **Bike Trecks** (T01539-431505, biketrecks.net).

What's your advice for a family visiting The Lakes?

Get out on the water. We're canoeists and since our children were very young we have paddled out for a picnic and a walk. Our favourite place is Watbarrow Point, a rocky outcrop from Windermere's west shore. It's about three miles southwest of Ambleside on the Wray Castle estate and very handy for the Low Wray campsite (see page 64). We take the ferry from Ambleside to the little jetty in Low Wray Bay. The more you can stay off the roads in summer, the better it is for everyone.

The kids love it as a place to play hide and seek. To me, it feels very magical. The west side of Windermere is generally quieter and Watbarrow Point still feels very calm. Even on a bank holiday, you can still find somewhere quiet.

Do you think each lake has its own unique character?

Windermere is my home lake. It has a drama about it, especially the views from the northern end. For me, Coniston has a certain tranquillity about it that the other lakes don't have. It feels different. The southern tip of Coniston feels like it's at the end of the world.

From being on the water and walking by the lakes, I can feel the character of each lake. Maybe it's a subconscious thing? Wastwater, for example, looks like a Norwegian fjord, while Ullswater has high fells on both sides and a kink in the middle.

Ambleside has been home for some 20-odd years. How can visitors feel at home despite the obvious changes?

Ambleside is a major hub for walkers. That gives the town a lively feel and the university campus there now also brings a sense of vibrancy to the place. More money coming into the town over the last 20 years has increased the quality and variety of shops, such as Gaynor Sports for outdoor equipment, and there are some great places today to eat, such as Lucy's. But what makes Ambleside still feel very Cumbrian to me is the sense of community.

As a parent, what are your personal top tips for families around the region?

I would always direct families towards Grizedale Forest for walking. I always find Grizedale engages kids in ways that other walks don't. And the Trust's Low Wray campsite is a winner for its lakeside location, biking trails and ferry access. It's that *Swallows and Amazons* experience – a way for families to get back to basics. There's nothing fluffy about it, but it's ideal for people who like tranquillity and nature.

Jo Haughton, Marketing Assistant for the National Trust.

Jo Haughton on Coniston Water.

Sleeping Central Lakes

Pick of the pitches

Castlerigg Hall Caravan and Camping Park

Keswick, CA12 4TE, T01768-774499, castlerigg.co.uk. Mar-Nov £6.30-7.50 adult, £2.90-3.85 child (5-15). Caravan pitches from £16.95; 4-berth holiday caravans from £240/week; family camping pods (sleeps 4) from £39 night.

Caravans and tents share lovely views over Derwentwater at this terraced site, which has a well-stocked shop, gleaming washrooms, games room and playing field. With an onsite café (great breakfasts) and a pub just outside the entrance, this is an ideal site for lazy campers, although you'll probably feel you've earned a meal out after hiking the 25-minute (steepish) walk down to Keswick and back a few times. Castlerigg Hall Caravan and Camping Park won the Holiday Park of the year award at the 2009 England's Northwest tourism awards ceremony. No reservations, so pitch up early to get the pick of the views.

Low Wray Campsite

Nr Ambleside, LA22 0JA, T01539-432810, ntlakescampsites.org.uk. Easter-Oct £4.50-5.50 adult, £2-2.50 child, £11-13.50 family, £3-3.50 vehicle.

One of three Cumbrian campsites owned by the National Trust, Low Wray is a beautiful site on the quiet western shore of Windermere. It is situated off the B5286 three miles southwest of Ambleside, and signposted from Clappersgate. This popular site offers the ultimate Lakeland camping idyll – the tent pitched next to a lake, canoes hauled up on a beach, and glorious views across fell and water. It's worth paying the £5 premium for a lakeside site and arriving at the reception promptly at 1200 when pitches are allocated on a first-come, first-served basis. And be sure to spend another £5 on midge repellent. The Drunken Duck Inn (see page 75), one of the Lake District's best pubs, is only a 10-minute drive away.

Park Cliffe Camping and Caravanning Estate

Windermere, T015395-31344, parkcliffe.co.uk. Mar-Nov £19.50-28/pitch (2 people), £5 extra adult, £2 extra child (5-17).

Combining fell-side camping with a few home comforts, Park Cliffe, situated about four miles north of Newby Bridge off the A590, is well equipped for family camping. A mixture of touring pitches and holiday caravans, the site has a restaurant, shop and immaculate washrooms. You can even hire a private bathroom for an extra £13 night. There are plenty of walks right on the doorstep, although kids will be happy enough messing about in the shallow beck that flows through the campsite. An overnight stay in the new camping pods costs £35 night.

Please note: Caravans and motor homes must approach Park Cliffe from the direction of Newby Bridge.

Syke Farm Campsite

Buttermere Village, CA13 9XA, T01768-770222. Year round £6 adult, £3 child.

Feeling intrepid? Good, because you won't find much in the way of mod cons at this wonderfully wild-and-woolly site. Wild because it's surrounded by the brooding peaks of Buttermere Fell, and woolly because you'll be sharing it with sheep. Rocky and undulating, it's not the best place to pitch up with an eight-berth super-tent. You also need to carry gear from the car park across a beck. In return, you'll get a stone hut with toilets and a couple of hot showers (50p a go), cold water for washing up and a picnic shelter. Family camping disaster in-the-making? Not if you like the no-frills approach with superb walking around Buttermere and Crummock Water thrown into the bargain. And kids will enjoy the flat walks around the shore plus Scale Force, the Lake District's highest waterfall on the other side of Crummock Water. Oh, and the delicious Syke Farm ice cream. As added incentives, the Fish Hotel and a farmhouse café serving cakes, scones and ice cream are a short stroll away.

Also recommended
Great Langdale Campsite
Langdale Valley, LA22 9JU, T01539-437668, ntlakescampsites.org.uk.
Year round, £4.50-5.50 adult, £2-2.50 child, £11-13.50 family, £20-35 camping pods, £250-410 yurts/week, £3-3.50/vehicle.
A delightfully remote and surprisingly popular National Trust-owned site with a selection of yurts (see page 23) and camping pods (see page 15) for a family 'glamping' trip.

Keswick Camping & Caravanning Club Site
Keswick, CA12 5EP, T01768-772392, campingandcaravanningclub.co.uk.
Feb-Nov £7.10-8.17 adult, £2.45-2.50 child, £19.38-20.21 family.
A tranquil lakeside campsite at the northern tip of Derwentwater and close to the town centre.

Walker Park Camping & Caravanning Club Site
Derwentwater, nr Keswick, CA12 5EN, T01768-772579, campingandcaravanningclub.co.uk.
May-Sep £5-8.10 adult, £2.50-2.70 child, £1.50-20.20 family.
A spacious, grassy site for caravans and motor homes but no tents on this site – head to the sister site in Keswick (above).

Cool & quirky

Four Winds Lakeland Tipis
Low Wray Campsite, nr Ambleside, 4windslakelandtipis.co.uk, T01539-821227. Apr-Nov 12-ft tipi (sleeps 2) from £270/week low season, £310/week high season, 18-ft Little World tipi (sleeps up to 6), from £390/week low season, £395/week high season.
Seven Native American tipis with raised wooden floors, made cosy with colourful rugs and cushions and equipped with gas cooker, full range of utensils, candle lanterns and more. The larger tipis include futons and outdoor picnic tables. It's currently located at Low Wray, but the camp moves between locations.

Full Circle
Rydal, lake-district-yurts.co.uk, T07975-671928. Year round, from £265/week off peak and £295/week peak season for a 5-day mid-week break. Each yurt sleeps up to 6 people with a double bed, 2 singles and room for 2 more to sleep on the floor.
Operates a select group of yurts at Rydal in the heart of the Lakes. Each authentic Mongolian *ger* has a wood-burning stove, lanterns, rugs and comfortable beds. There's an excellent adventure playground, plus streams, woods and waterfalls.

Lakeland Campers
Croft Foot Farm, nr Kendal, LA8 0DF, T01539-824357, lakelandcampers. co.uk. Jun-Sep from £495/week, Sep-Oct £450/week, plus £150 non-refundable deposit.
Make way for Dolly the Van, a 1969 type-2 Volkswagen camper van sleeping four. It has been very well restored and has added extras for the 21st-century camping experience. Optional extras include bedding hire (£10), a drive-away awning to sleep four (£15) and a BBQ kit (£15). You can even follow Dolly the Van on Twitter.

Rainbow Camper Hire
Keswick, CA12 5QB, T01768-780413, vwcamperhire.net. Year round, from £500-650/week, £295-350/3 nights.
Who will you pick from this line-up of classic 1970s VW campers? Maisie and Daisy are the obvious family choices with room for two adults and up to four kids; Fleur sleeps up to four and has a flower-power paint job, while four-berth Billy Bling is decked out in chrome and has flashy extras like a PlayStation and digital TV. There's also a host of optional extras to hire, such as a bike carrier (£15) and bedding hire (£15).

Sleeping Central Lakes

Fallbarrow Park

Bowness-on-Windermere, T01539-444422, slholidays.co.uk. Call for offers.
Tucked away between the trees on the eastern shore of Windermere, this tranquil spot has lodges and cottages as well as the usual caravans you would expect from a holiday park group with six locations in the region. The facilities for families are top-notch with a laundry, a kids' multi-activity play area and a smart new deli-café with Wi-Fi internet access. But don't bother to bring your tent – this is a camping-free zone.

Kendal Youth Hostel

Kendal, T0845-371 9641, yha.org.uk. Year round, from £15.95 adult, £54.95 family.
This hostel is a bit frayed around the edges but it is a great central base next to the Brewery Arts Centre (see page 74). Family rooms are spacious with comfy bunks, and rates include a cooked breakfast. There's also a TV room and members' kitchen.

Monkhouse Hill Cottages

Nr Caldbeck, CA5 7HW, T016974-76254, monkhousehill.co.uk. £475-815/week (4-6 bed cottage).
Luxury self catering, with free membership of the North Lakes Spa and lots of extras for children – especially pre-school.

Regent by the Lake

Ambleside, LA22 0ES, T015394-32254, regentlakes.co.uk. Year round, rates vary; phone for details of packages.
A small hotel with a fabulous location on Windermere's Waterhead Bay. There are spacious family rooms (with PlayStations), an indoor heated pool and a restaurant that is well known for its organic Cumbrian cuisine.

Windermere Marina Village

Bowness-on-Windermere, LA23 3JQ, T01539-446551, wmv.com. Cottages from £395/week, £320/short break, apartments from £325/week, £320/short break. Call ahead for special deals.
This peaceful marina village complex, a 15-minute drive south

of Bowness-on-Windermere, on the A592, offers self-catering accommodation and a good range of facilities in a secluded setting. The standard of accommodation is high, making for a self-contained base, while an onsite shop and café-bar-cum-swimming pool complex add to the appeal. Ask at reception to hire cots and high chairs and to collect free electricity socket safety discs. Overall, it makes for a welcome break from the frenzy of the town centre.

YHA Ambleside

Ambleside, LA22 0EU, T0845-3719620, yha.org.uk. Year round from £37.95/3-bed family room, £67.95/6-bed family room, plus breakfast £4.65 adult, £2.95 child.
A flagship property in the YHA portfolio, this modern, lakeside hostel has excellent facilities, including an appealing restaurant. You can also hire canoes and sit-on kayaks for some fun on Lake Windermere. The hostel is located right next to Ambleside Pier, offering easy access around the region.

YHA Keswick

Keswick, T0845-371 9746, yha.org.uk. Year round, dorms £15.95 adult, £11.95 child.
A newly refurbished hostel with top-notch facilities and a great in-house café (open 1100-1700). It has great riverside views of the River Greta.

Farm favourites

Ashness Farm
Borrowdale, nr Keswick, CA12 5UN, T01768-777361, ashnessfarm.co.uk.
Five B&B rooms and superb views of Derwentwater.

Fornside Farm Cottages
St John's in the Vale, nr Keswick, CA12 4TS, T01768-779173, fornside.co.uk.
Four barn conversions (sleeping four to six) on a working sheep farm with spectacular views of the Helvellyn Range.

High Loanthwaite Farm
Outgate, nr Ambleside, LA22 0NL, T01539-436279, lakedistrictfarmhouse.co.uk.
A 16th-century period farmhouse with two B&B rooms and an open fire.

High Wray Farm
High Wray, nr Ambleside, LA22 0JE, T01539-432280, highwrayfarm.co.uk.
Three cosy, homely rooms in a rural setting.

Hollows Farm
Grange, nr Keswick, CA12 5UQ, T01768-777298, hollowsfarm.co.uk.
Three B&B rooms in a 17th-century farmhouse, near the picturesque hamlet of Grange, with breakfast cooked on the Aga. Also offers homely self-catering cottage for two; no pets or smoking.

Moor Farm
Castlerigg, nr Keswick, CA12 4TE, T01768-773022, moorfarmkeswick.co.uk.
A 300-year-old stone-built farmhouse just a short stroll to the Castlerigg Stone Circle (see page 33). Three cosy B&B rooms.

Seatoller Farm Cottage
Borrowdale, nr Keswick, CA12 5XN, T01768-777232, seatollerfarm.co.uk.
A cosy self-catering cottage sleeping four, located at the foot of the Honister Pass; great for walking and touring.

Side House Farm and Cottages
Great Langdale, nr Ambleside, LA22 9JU, T01539-437364, millbeckfarm.co.uk.
Two self-catering cottages, one sleeping six and the other three, on a working hill farm.

Yew Tree Farm
Coniston, LA21 8DP, T01539-441433, yewtree-fram.com.
Three upscale B&B rooms in the farmhouse used in the film, *Miss Potter*, adjoining the famous tearoom (see page 70).

Sleeping Central Lakes

Also recommended

Bank Ground Farm

Coniston, LA21 8AA, T01539-441264, bankground.com.

Five homely self-catering cottages are available for hire alongside the farmhouse B&B and tearoom. The location inspired Arthur Ransome's *Swallows and Amazons*.

Butharlyp Howe YHA

Grasmere, T0845-371 9746, yha.org.uk. Feb-Nov daily, Dec-Jan weekends.

Superior, modern hostel set in a charming period mansion with good facilities and family rooms.

Cote How Organic Guesthouse

Rydal, nr Ambleside, LA22 9LW, T01539-432765, cotehow.co.uk.

One of just three organic guesthouses in the UK that are licensed by the Soil Association.

Storrs Gate House

Bowness-on-Windermere, LA23 3JD, T01539-443272, storrsgatehouse. co.uk.

Winner of the Cumbria Tourism Award for Bed and Breakfast of the Year 2009.

Waterwheel

Ambleside, LA22 9DU, T01539-433286, waterwheelambleside.co.uk.

Smart and upmarket with port and Kendal Mint Cake awaiting your arrival in all three cottage-style rooms. Better suited to older children.

Yewfield

Hawkshead Hill, LA22 0PR, T01539-436765, yewfield.co.uk.

Self-catering cottages and an upscale B&B famed for its vegetarian breakfast.

Splashing out

Angel Inn

Bowness-on-Windermere, LA23 3BU, T01539-444080, the-angelinn.com. From £110 room B&B/weekend, £90 room B&B/mid-week (£22.50 child sharing, £10 cot). Call ahead for special deals.

A chic, contemporary hotel with a firm family-friendly policy, the Angel has been carefully thought out and is well equipped. The 14 rooms are modern and comfy. Most of these are in the main house, although families may prefer the quieter annex rooms in the Gatehouse. Serves good food too (see page 74).

Castle Green Hotel

Kendal LA9 6RG, T015395-734000, castlegreen.co.uk. Year round from £69 doubles, £89 family B&B.

Located just west of Kendal and set in leafy grounds with views across to Kendal Castle, this upscale hotel has large family rooms for up to five people. Options for in-house dining include the more formal

Greenhouse restaurant and a steakhouse-cum-pub with local ales. There is a generous breakfast buffet with healthy options. Use of the Pulse Leisure Club, which has a pool and gym, is included in the rate for guests.

Howbeck Windermere Suites

Windermere, LA23 2LA, T01539-444739, howbeck.co.uk. From £100 room/B&B, plus £10 child sharing. Call ahead for special deals.

A new addition to the boutique Howbeck Hotel, the smart but homely Windermere Suites offer apartment-style rooms two doors away from the main hotel. Three of the suites, Bowness, Ambleside and Coniston, are suitable for children and have private patio space. Breakfast is served direct to the room.

Langdale Hotel and Country Club

Great Langdale, LA22 9JD, T01539-437302; langdale.co.uk. From £725/week (2-bedroom chalet with additional sofa bed). From £100 doubles at the hotel/B&B.

Set in a gorgeous 35-acre estate, Langdale combines the top-notch facilities of a hotel – three restaurants (takeaways too), swimming pool and spa – with 80 Scandinavian-style chalets for timeshare or rental. The grounds include streams, tarns and other water features.

Lodore Falls Hotel

Keswick, CA12 5UX, T01768-777285, lakedistricthotels.net. From £108 doubles, £163 two-room suites/B&B. Part of the family-oriented Lake District Hotels Group, the Lodore Falls is a stately property with a good range of facilities, albeit with a slightly old-fashioned feel. Family rooms easily accommodate two extra beds, while the two-room suites are worth the extra for the lounge and separate bedroom provided. Facilities include a pool, free bike hire (returnable deposit payable) for both adults and kids, children's menus and high chairs, and a children's film club. Parents can seek refuge with a sundowner at the nightly sunset cocktail session on the terrace overlooking Derwentwater. Located on the B5289 three miles southeast of Keswick, and just across the road from the Lodore jetty for the Keswick Launch (see page 44).

Riverside Hotel

Kendal LA9 6EL, T01539-734861; riversidekendal.co.uk. Doubles weekends/mid-week £108/98 B&B. The nearest hotel to Kendal's train station is looking a bit smarter since a recent refurbishment swept away the tired old fittings. Children under three stay free, while special rates for children sharing with parents are also available – call for details.

Waterhead Hotel

Ambleside, LA22 0ER, T01539-432566, elh.co.uk. From £106/house room B&B, £152/luxury room B&B, plus £20 child sharing.

A smart and contemporary townhouse hotel right beside Ambleside Pier, the Waterhead offers upscale facilities and lots of contemporary touches. Cots and high chairs are supplied on demand, while guests receive a pass for the leisure club at its sister hotel, Low Wood, located one mile away. The rooms are divided into three categories, with prices to match; the top-end Luxury Rooms offer lake views and extra space to fit in cots or additional beds. Overall the Waterhead is a stylish option.

Also recommended
Gilpin Lodge Country House Hotel

Windermere, LA23 3NE, T01539-488818, gilpinlodge.co.uk.

Harwood Hotel

Grasmere, LS22 9SP, T01539-435248, harwoodhotel.co.uk.

Moss Grove Hotel Organic

Grasmere, LA22 9SW, T01539-435251, mossgrove.com.

White Moss House Hotel

Rydal Water, nr Grasmere, LA22 9SE, T015394-35295, whitemoss.com.

Eating Central Lakes

Local goodies

Grasmere Gingerbread Shop

Grasmere, T01539-435428,
grasmeregingerbread.co.uk.
Year round Mon-Sat 0915-1730,
Sun 1230-1730.
The recipe for Sarah Nelson's
famous gingerbread has been
a closely guarded secret for
more than 150 years (the recipe
is apparently locked in a bank
vault). You can't buy the rib-
sticking gingerbread anywhere

Tuck into a slice of history

Nibbled and sucked by Chris
Bonnington on the summit of
Everest in May 1953, Romney's
Kendal Mint Cake (kendal.
mintcake.co.uk) is still going
strong, though purists might
argue that new-fangled
buttermint and chocolate
varieties are just for softies.
There are three manufacturers
in Kendal: Wilsons, Quiggins and
Romney's, who bought out the
original manufacturer, Wipers, in
1930. Sadly, visits to the factories
are ruled out on health and safety
grounds these days, but Kendal's
tourist information centre still
does a roaring trade in mint-
cake bars. Stock up on supplies
between browsing the brochures.

Kendal Mint Cake.

else and it remains a bestseller.
The tiny shop was originally
the village schoolhouse, built
in 1630, and a place where
Wordsworth occasionally taught.
Today a visit to the world-
famous shop is a treat in itself
with ladies in starched aprons
busying themselves behind
the counter and surly chefs
emerging, sweating, from the
kitchen. Expect big queues.

Low Sizergh Barn

Nr Kendal LA8 8DZ, T01539-560426,
lowsizerghbarn.co.uk. Year round
daily 0900-1730.
More than simply a farm shop
(although it is a rather good one
with every Cumbrian speciality
imaginable), Low Sizergh is an
ideal lunch spot for families, on
the A591 a mile south of Kendal.
You can watch the cows being
milked in the yard (daily around
1315), then head downstairs to
the craft shop, or upstairs to the
café for tasty lunches with daily
specials – try the home-made
lemonade (£1.85). Then walk off
lunch on the organic farm trail, a
1¾-mile route plotted on a free
map available from the shop.

Lucy's Specialist Grocers

Ambleside, LA22 9DJ, T01539-
432288, lucysofambleside.co.uk.
Year round daily 0900-2100.
A local foodie phenomenon,
Lucy's is part of an empire
stretching across the Central
Lakes. You can now even enrol
on Family Fun Day courses at

Market days

Kendal Market Place, farmers'
market last Friday of month and
Saturday market.
Keswick Saturday market and
Thursday craft market.

Lucy Cooks Cookery School
(Staveley, T01539-432288,
lucycooks.co.uk, courses from
£105/2 people, £210/family
of 4). But it's the deli where it
all started back in 1989, and
it's still here that you'll find
an Aladdin's Cave of breads,
pastries, chutneys, cheeses and
meals-to-go, including Lucy's
Sublime Sticky Toffee Pudding.
Stop by for freshly made
baguettes and sandwiches, or
stock up on speciality hampers
and gluten-free goodies. It's a
great place to whip up a tasty
picnic – although you may
never leave. See also Lucy's
on a Plate, page 74.

Yew Tree Farm

Coniston, LA21 8DP, T01539-441433,
yewtree-farm.com, heritagemeats.
co.uk. Easter-Oct daily for lunches
and afternoon teas, Nov-Apr
weekends and holidays 1100-1600.
Farm-fresh heritage meats on
sale at this well-liked farmhouse
B&B (page 67) and café (page 73)
include Belted Galloway beef
and Herdwick lamb. The animals
are reared on mixed grassland
or heather fells, are not given
antibiotics, and are treated
humanely from birth to slaughter.

The hampers, using all parts of the animal, start from £65 for a Cook Delight Beltie Box to £90 for a Speciality Herdwick Hamper.

Also recommended
Hawkshead Relish Company
Hawkshead, T01539-436614, hawksheadrelish.com. Mon-Sat 0930-1700, Sun 1000-1700.
Award-winning chutneys, relishes and mustards – the perfect accompaniment to a board of local cheeses.

Heidi's of Grasmere
Grasmere, T01539-435248, harwoodhotel.co.uk.
Tucked under the Harwood Hotel in Grasmere's Red Lion Square, Heidi's has chutneys, salsas and delicatessen-style snacks. See also the Harwood Hotel, page 69.

Plumgarth Farm Shop
Lakelands Food Park, Kendal LA8 8LX, T01539-736300, plumgarths.co.uk.

Also in Kendal, **Staff of Life** (T01539-738606, artisanbreadmakers.co.uk) for fresh bread and **Baba Ganoush** (T01539-731072) for delicatessen dips. Both are situated next to Pots of Love, see page 57.

Quick & simple

Apple Pie
Ambleside, T015394-33679, applepieambleside.co.uk.
Year round daily 0900-1700.
You may arrive at this central Ambleside café with one thing on your mind – apple pie made with mixed spice and sultanas, served with a dollop of Windermere Ice Cream (£3.45), but you'll soon notice other goodies, like the chocolate-coated Fell Top Choc Flapjack (92p) and you might wonder if you've got room for a taste of the Cumberland sausage, cider and potato pie (£2.78) – well, it would be rude not to, really. And chances are that once you've over-indulged in the courtyard

The Apple Pie, Ambleside.

café and taken advantage of the free Wi-Fi in the Green Room, you will be stocking up on picnic rolls, pies and pasties from the adjoining bakery counter.

Bluebird Café

Coniston Boating Centre, T01539-441649, thebluebirdcafe.co.uk. Feb-Nov daily 1000-1700; Dec-Jan Sat-Sun 1030-1630.
Named after Donald Campbell's famous boat, this toes-in-the-water café is filled with memorabilia about his various water-speed record-breaking attempts on Coniston Water. It was originally built as accommodation for the crew of the steam yacht *Gondola* (see page 45), which sails from just outside the café even today. Popular hot bites include Cumberland sausage butty

with apple sauce (£3.70), and there are soups, sandwiches, salads and jacket potatoes. When the *Gondola* shows up, the sunny terrace soon echoes to the sound of clinking tea cups and contented munching on the house-special chocolate brownies (£2.05).

Famous 1657 Chocolate House

Kendal, T01539-740702, chocolatehouse1657.co.uk. Year round daily 0900-1700.
Kids love chocolate, and parents will love this place too. Head upstairs to the café for 18 types of hot chocolate and souvenir gift boxes of classy chocs (including gluten-free options), then downstairs for take-away Peter Rabbit chocolates and souvenir sweets.

Farrer's Tea & Coffee House

Kendal, T01539-731709, farrersofkendal.co.uk. Year round daily 0900-1700.
Caffeine fix ahoy. There's been a coffee shop here since 1819 and the creaky, labyrinthine building dates from 1640. Sipping a shot of Farrer's Number One blend (£1.75) on the pavement of Stricklandgate is the ideal way to watch bustling Kendal go about its business.

Good Taste Café

Keswick, T01768-775973, simplygoodtaste.co.uk. Year round daily 0900-1700.
The domain of local chef Peter Sidwell is a charmingly simple

Famous 1657 Chocolate House, Kendal.

Fish & chips

Picture the scene: hot chips and crispy battered fish steaming in newspaper, little wooden forks, salt, vinegar and a pickle, maybe some mushy peas. If your mouth's watering already, then head to Cumbria's best traditional chippy. The **Old Keswickian** (Keswick, T01768-773861, oldkeswickian. co.uk) has become a landmark for its fish suppers and home-made pies. There is a children's menu for under-eights.
Also worth trying are **The Little Chippy**, Windermere, and the **Walnut Fish Bar**, Ambleside.

❸ There are now an estimated 8500 fish and chip shops across the UK – that's eight for every one Golden Arches. Take that Ronald McDonald!

but hearty place for lunchtime snacks and afternoons teas. This is no bog-standard café, however. The emphasis is on high quality local produce, freshly prepared with imagination and served on slate slabs. Head upstairs for sink-into sofas and a box of toys to keep children busy during the wait. Many of the dishes are documented in Sidwell's book *Simply Good Taste: Great Food from the Lake District* (Simon & Schuster, £14).

Jumble Room

Grasmere, T01539-435188, thejumbleroom.co.uk. Lunch Wed-Sun 1200-1500, dinner Wed-Mon from 1800.
A relic of the Seventies hippy trail in tourist-central Grasmere? This funky, jazzy, arty café has more throws and scatter cushions than a Moroccan bazaar and a funky menu to boot with lunch mains priced £9-13, dinner mains £13-24. Or you could just pop in for an espresso and a taste of life in a far-off land. On a quiet side street off the main square.

Lazy Daisy's Lakeland Kitchen

Windermere, T01539-443877, lazydaisyslakelandkitchen.co.uk. Year round 0930-2100 (dinner menu from 1700).
An old-school traditional family café in the hands of a dedicated foodie and local produce

champion. The menu changes according to the time of day, but all feature good vegetarian dishes, local fish and meat and hearty kids' options. The children's lunch, priced at £5.95, includes a drink and an ice cream. The weekly pudding club is close to nirvana for the sweet-toothed (£4.25).

Waterhead Coffee Shop

Ambleside, T01539-432028. Year round, daily 0900-1700.
A cute little coffee shop, part of the Waterhead Hotel (see page 69), on the Ambleside foreshore. It's a handy spot for coffee while you wait for the next boat. In fact, it's worth missing the boat for the calorie-laden house special, the Hot Choc Dip. The drawback? No toilets. Head across the road to the public ones by the pay-and-display car park – but don't expect nappy-changing facilities.

Waterside Wholefoods

Kendal, T01539-729743. Year round 0900-1700.
A tranquil location on the riverside overlooking Miller Bridge, and a menu of vegetarian and health foods. Expect organic, fair-trade and local produce served with a smile. The café noticeboard is the clarion call for the local alternative community.

Yew Tree Farm

Coniston, LA21 8DP, T01539-441433, yewtree-farm.com. Easter-Oct daily for lunches and afternoon teas, Nov-Apr weekends and holidays 1100-1600.
This 600-acre working farm doubled for Hill Top in the film *Miss Potter*, the 2006 Hollywood take on the Beatrix Potter story starring Renee Zellweger. Situated off the A593 and B5285 1½ miles north of Coniston, it is a superb place to stop for lunch. There's a daily lunch special for around £5 and the home-baked cheddar scones with chutney (£3.50) are a perennial favourite. Kids can play wth the toys in the front room or the mini tractor outside. There are even lambs, puppies and chickens to provide a mid-lunch cabaret of cute farm animals. Five-star accommodation with a full farmer's breakfast is available in three tasteful rooms in the 17th-century farmhouse (prices from £112/night). See also pages 67 and 70.

Zeffirellis

Ambleside, T01539-433845, zeffirellis.com. Café daily from 1000, restaurant daily from 1730.
This restaurant, café, jazz bar and cinema in the centre of Ambleside is buzzing most evenings. Book in advance to eat great pizzas (around £9), Mediterranean-inspired mains (around £10; £4.25 for a child-sized serving) followed by a movie, or accompanied by some live jazz. Pasta and puds are also

available, while the daytime café serves quiche, soup, jacket potatoes and cakes, as well as the full pizza menu. Vegetarian families should make a beeline for the new sister property, **Fellinis** (T01539-432487), which is located just across town. Both places have a Meal Offer – two courses and a ticket for the next screening priced at £17.95 for Zeffirellis and £19.95 at Fellinis.

Also recommended
Black Bull Inn
Coniston, T01539-441335, conistonbrewey.com.
Decent pub grub and a pint of award-winning ale, including Bluebird and Coniston Old Man, from Coniston's much-loved microbrewery.

Lighthouse
Windermere, T01539-488260.
Year round daily from 0900 to late.
This European-style café-bar is a lively spot, spilling out onto the pavement on sunny days. Sit downstairs for light bites and coffees, or choose a spot across the two upper floors for dinner or drinks, with bistro mains priced £10-15.

Norman's Café
Ambleside, T01539-431198.
Year round daily 1000-1630.
A simple and central café, Norman's includes an indoor soft play centre. Look out for the Play & Eat deal (£5), or the Play & Drink option (£3).

Pheasant Inn
Bassenthwaite, T017687-76234, the-pheasant.co.uk. Year round daily from 1200.
A traditional coaching inn serving lunch, afternoon teas and upmarket dinners.

Watermill Inn
Ings, nr Windermere, T01539-821309; watermillinn.co.uk.
Founded as an add-on to the family pub, the microbrewery produces around 6300 pints of local ale per week. Bar meals all day with mains around £12. Very dog friendly.

Wilf's Café
Staveley, T01539-822329, wilfs-cafe.co.uk. Year round Mon-Fri from 1000, Sat-Sun from 0930.
A riverside café with good snack-style food, a sunny terrace and a children's area.

Posh nosh

Angel Inn
Bowness-on-Windermere, T01539-444080, the-angelinn.com. Daily lunch and dinner.
The sign says it all: eat, drink, sleep, child and baby friendly. The Angel is indeed heavenly, combining multi-purpose facilities and gastropub food. The brunches are tasty, the all-day cold sandwiches and hot wraps (£5-7.50) filling and the evening mains (£10-20) include a succulent fell-bred, aged steak. Even the kids' meals

(around £5) are good enough for an adult. For children, there's a goody bag upon arrival, high chairs and a box of books and toys in the conservatory, where most families tend to sit if the garden is rained off. All this, and Bluebird ale on draught from the Coniston Brewery.

Brewery Arts Centre
Kendal, T01539-725133, breweryarts.co.uk.
The Intro Bar next to the Brewery's box office is a buzzy café with a play area for toddlers. Other options include the Vats Bar upstairs, relaxed, with a daily pizza menu (around £8) and bar snacks, and the Grain Store Restaurant next-door, a smarter option for dining in style – around £20 for three courses. An excellent all-rounder in great surroundings.

Lucy's on a Plate
Ambleside, T01539-431191, lucysofambleside.co.uk.
Daily 1000-2100.
Champion of Cumbrian produce Lucy Nicholson has built a foodie empire and this bustling café-restaurant remains the linchpin of her fiefdom. The huge menu sprawls over several pages and is peppered with word play, such as the Give Us a Strog Fungi and the Trout and About. There's a specials menu served until 1700 each day (£12 for two courses) and a kids' menu (up to 12 years)

with prices around £5. There are also colouring books in the conservatory (the best area for families), high chairs and nappy-changing facilities upstairs. But, despite giving the impression of world domination, Lucy's has been accused of spreading her empire too thinly. In fact, the menu pre-empts complaints of slow service by bidding diners to relax into the local rhythm.

See also **Lucy4 Wine Bar & Bistro** (Ambleside, T01539-434666; Bowness-on-Windermere T01539-442793, daily 1700-2300 for tapas £5-8) and **LucyBytes Café** (Ambleside, T01539-432223) for snacks and cakes.

Masons Arms
Bowland Bridge, nr Bowness-on-Windermere, T015395-68486, masonsarmsstrawberrybank.co.uk. Daily lunch and dinner.
Overlooking Winster Valley near Lake Windermere, this is one of the region's best pubs, serving wholesome dishes, such as Lakeland pork and damson sausages with mash and onion gravy (£11.95) and Grasmere gingerbread and rhubarb crumble (£5.25).

Rococo Joes
Kendal, T01539-734655, rococojoes.co.uk. Tue-Sat 1000-2300, Sun from 1600.
Home-made pizzas (around £8) are the main draw at this central family favourite in Kendal. It

boasts high chairs and a kids' menu, and there are more adventurous toppings for the parents.

White House
Bowness-on-Windermere, T01539-444803, whitehouse-lakedistrict.co.uk. Daily lunch and dinner.
Tucked away on Lowside in Bowness, this informal bar, café and terrace offers good-value set menus (£10/15 for 2/3 courses), including decent vegetarian options, but only if you eat early. Otherwise mains range from £8-16 and include tasty local dishes, such as venison cooked in stout. The surroundings are modern and contemporary with lots of private tables hidden behind beams and pillars.

Also recommended
Drunken Duck Inn
Barngate, nr Ambleside, T01539-436347, drunkenduckinn.co.uk.
A renowned gastropub and chic B&B for top-notch meals washed down with a pint of cask ale from the in-house Barngates Brewery.

Francine's Coffee House and Restaurant
Windermere, T01539-444088, francinesrestaurant windermere.co.uk.
This popular Windermere bistro-style restaurant has daily specials and great local seafood specials.

Glass House
Ambleside, T01539-432137, theglasshouserestaurant.co.uk.
This central Ambleside eatery is back in business after one of Gordon Ramsay's legendary tirades on *Ramsay's Kitchen Nightmares* TV series. Check out the Next Generation menu for under-12s.

Raise a glass to parents

Cumbria has enjoyed a rich heritage of artisan brewing since the 1830 Beer Act first gave rise to a proliferation of local brewhouses. The popularity of real ale hit a low point in the 1970s, but today Cumbria boasts over 20 of the UK's 600-odd independent breweries. One of the best is **Hawkshead Brewery** (Staveley, T01539-825269, hawksheadbrewery.co.uk, year round 1200-1700), which is on the Lakes Line Real Ale Trail. A green-friendly initiative collaboratively launched by Westmorland CAMRA and the Lakes Lines Community Rail Partnership, the trail highlights pubs, breweries and eateries along the rural Lakes Line from the mainline train hub of Oxenholme to Windermere via Kendal. Cheers!

View from the Drunken
Duck Inn, near Ambleside.

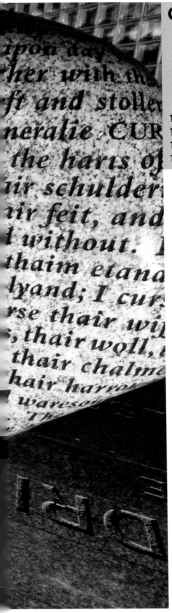

Tullie House.

Contents

North & East Lakes

SCOTLAND

Chapelknowe
Newton
Gretna
Stapleton
Longtown
Kirklinton
Kirkcambeck
West Hall
Birdoswald Roman Fort
Wiley Sike
Gilsland
Boltonfellend
Smithfield
West Linton
Scaleby
Newtown
Walton
Course of Hadrian's Wall
Banks
Lanercost Priory
Low Row
Todhills
Rockliffe
Harker
A World in Miniature Museum
Walby Farm Park
Brampton
Milton
Hallbankgate
Bowness-on-Solway
Burgh-by-Sands
Beaumont
Crosby-on-Eden
Hayton
Talkin Tarn Country Park
Glasson
Drumburgh
Linstock
Warwick Bridge
Castle Carrock
Cold Fell (621 m)
Kirkbride
Moorhouse
Stanwix
Tullie House
Carlisle
Morton
Wetheral
King's Forest
Wiggonby
Great Orton
Cummwhitton
Baldwinholme
Cotehill
Cumwhitton
Thursby
Buckabank
Wreay
Holmwrangle
Newbiggin
Wigton
Brackenthwaite
Raughton Head
High Head Sculpture Valley
High Hesket
Armathwaite
Croglin
Rosley
Welton
Old Town
Renwick
Brocklebank
Sebergham
Ivegill
Hay Close Maize
High Bankhill
Caldbeck
Hesket Newmarket
Thomas Close
Low Braithwaite
Inglewood Forest
Hutton End
Lazonby
Branthwaite
Millhouse
Ellonby
Unthank
Plumpton
Great Salkeld
Melmerby
High Pike (658 m)
Mosedale
Johnby
Upfront Gallery & Puppet Theatre
Newton Reigny
Winskill
Ousby
Knott (710 m)
Eden Ostrich World
Langwathby
Skirwith
Bassenthwaite
Greystoke
Berrier
Newbiggin
Edenhall
Culgaith
Newbiggin
Milburn
Great Calva (690 m)
Mungrisdale
Motherby
Fair Hill
Penrith
Dufton Fell
Applethwaite
Scales
Troutbeck
Stainton
Alpaca Centre
Eamont Bridge
Brougham
Silverband Falconry
Knock
Keswick
Threlkeld
Hutton
Sockbridge
Clifton
Melkinthorpe
Kirkby Thore
Dufton
Wreay
Pooley Bridge
Lowther
Cliburn
Brampton
Crackenthorpe
Matterdale End
Longthwaite
Askham
Morland
Hilton
Derwent Water
Watermillock
Knotts
Helton
Whale
Newby
Appleby-in-Westmorland
Great Ormside
Dowthwaitehead
Ullswater
Howtown
Bampton
Burrells
Hoff
Stanah
Fisher Place
Sandwick
Bampton Grange
Maulds Meaburn
Great Asby
Warcop
Thirlmere
Lake District National Park
Glenridding
Patterdale
Dale Head
Rosgill
Crosby Ravensworth
Great Musgrave
Rosthwaite
Helvellyn (949 m)
Bridgend
Haweswater
Shap
Keld
Soulby
Wythburn
Hartsop
Crosby Garrett
Kirkby Stephen
Wythburn Fells
Newbiggin-on-Lune
Nateb
Kirkstone Pass Inn
Orton
Ambleside
Tebay
Ravenstonedale

5 km
5 miles
N

A21
A75
A74
B6071
A6071
A689
A69
B5307
A595
A596
A595
B5299
M6
B5305
B5299
B5305
B6413
B6413
B6412
A66
A5091
A592
A66
A592
A591
A591
A5322
A6
A685
B6318
39
40
41
42
43
44
38
22
21

Rock carvings at Armathwaite, Eden Valley.

The first thing you notice about this part of the Lake District is the sky. As the M6 heads north, the industrial northwest gives way to an overriding sense of space, fresh air and awe-inspiring, region-defining wide-open skies. To the west, grumbling drivers and increasingly fidgety children may be stuck in traffic jams in the Lake District National Park. But all you can see is the empty road stretching far ahead, rolling fells on either side and your own private display of towering cumulonimbus. Welcome to the North and East Lakes, 1000-acre-sky country.

This area of Cumbria feels very different from the classic Lake District of the centre or the popular haunts of the south. The accent is stronger, the landscape wilder and the influence of neighbouring Scotland, Pennine Yorkshire and Northumberland all the stronger. But it's no less compelling as a place to visit. In fact, invest some of your precious holiday time in getting to know the area and you'll soon be won over by its rough-round-the-edges character.

Carlisle is the obvious starting point as it serves as the regional capital and a major transport hub. But while the town offers an attractive cathedral quarter and an ancient castle, it's the countryside around Carlisle that makes a lasting impression on visitors. The chocolate-box villages along the roads running northeast towards Hadrian's Wall ooze bucolic charm, while the wall itself, centred on **Birdoswald Roman Fort**, is a must-visit day out for any family with a child of school age – Roman Britain being part of the National Curriculum.

In the south of the region, **Penrith** is a perfect example of a busy Cumbrian market town and a good place to stock up on supplies, collect armfuls of brochures from the tourist information centre and indulge a sweet tooth in some local fudge made by royal appointment. But again it's the countryside around Penrith that begs to be explored. In particular, the **Eden Valley** is a little-known gem of rural northern Britain that most visitors pass by. And don't miss the attractive village of **Kirkby Stephen** – voted England's Best Village in 2009, and a jewel of the North and East Lakes. Meanwhile the crowds will be bombing down the A66 to **Whinfell Forest Center Parcs** – arguably the best Center Parcs in the country. But don't follow the crowd: instead, set the Sat Nav, take your time and go in search of your very own Garden of Eden.

Out & about North & East Lakes

Fun & free

Picnic by a lake

A rural 165-acre site, comprising a lake, mature woodland trails and peaceful flower-strewn meadows, Talkin Tarn Country Park (Talkin, nr Brampton, CA8 1HN) is an ideal place to relax and reconnect with nature. It is located two miles south of Brampton on the B6413 Castle Carrock road. A 1½-mile circular walk is accessible for buggies and wheelchairs, while three way-marked trails lead off into the forest. Back by the lake, there's a small adventure playground, a boathouse where you can hire rowing boats (£4 an hour) and a tearoom for soft drinks and coffees (daily 1030-1600). Best of all, Talkin is an ideal spot to take a picnic, settle down under a shady tree and watch the wildlife – otters, roe deer and red squirrels. Parking is a bargain £1 all day.

Go on a nature trail

Near Penrith, Cowraik Quarry is an abandoned sandstone

⊕ Clifton Moor, near Penrith, was the site of the last battle between Scottish and English armies to be fought on English soil. It took place on 18 December 1745. The dead from both sides are buried in the village of Clifton – the English in the churchyard, and the Scots under an oak tree (known as the Rebel Tree) at the end of Town End Croft, where a plaque marks the spot.

Kirkby Stephen train station.

Way out

KIRKBY STEPHEN

Explore England's Best Village

Kirkby Stephen, located at the head of the Eden Valley, was voted England's Best Village by Calor (www.calorvillageoftheyear.org) in 2009. Deservedly so. It's a delightful place to explore, with a raft of facilities (post office, supermarket, two pubs, bakery, two chip shops and free parking), plus lots of walking and cycling trails within easy striking distance of the central Market Square.

Head to the tourist information centre on Market Square (T01768-371199, visiteden. co.uk, year round Mon-Sat 1000-1600, Easter-Oct Sun 1100-1500, Oct-Mar Sat 1000-1200) to pick up free **maps** of local trails. Follow the **Town Trail** to take in the old church cloisters and the butter market, stopping off at the Appleby Bakery for fresh rolls, or the Mulberry Bush Café for a 'breakfast packet' (a huge, filled bread cake). The Book Shop (closed Tue and Thu) has lots of children's books and Little Treasures (closed Thu and Sun) has a wide range of children's clothes.

On the fringes of Kirkby Stephen, the **Poetry Path** is a circular walk for young children, with 12 poems carved in stone along the way, celebrating a year in the life of a hill farmer.

Further afield, several **cycling routes** take in the glorious countryside of the Eden Valley, which spans the Cumbrian Fells and the Pennines. Of these, the best for families with older children is the Mallerstang and Pendragon Castle Route, a 12½-mile on-road circular trail from Kirkby Stephen. This is mostly on rural B roads, although one section takes the A683 and extra caution is needed.

For walkers, there are two **circular walks** through the Crossbank Nature Reserve, both starting from the Fat Lamb pub (fatlamb. co.uk), at Ravenstonedale, just southwest of Kirkby Stephen. The 3½-mile trail follows ancient footpaths and crosses Scandal Beck before returning to the Fat Lamb, where you can have a pub lunch.

Out & about North & East

quarry on Beacon Hill, which supplied much of the red sandstone used to build the town's Victorian houses. Since the quarry closed, nature has reclaimed the site and it has become a designated nature reserve; a way-marked trail describes features of interest. You can park in the layby at the

Rheged Centre, Penrith,
main entrance and play area.

bottom of the track leading to the quarry; pick up a leaflet from the tourist information centre in Penrith.

Escape the rain
Beat those rainy-day blues at the **Rheged Centre** (Penrith, CA11 0DQ, T01768-868000, rheged.com, daily 1000-1700), located just off the M6, junction 40. It has shops and cafés specializing in local produce, a soft play area, a giant cinema screen and regular exhibitions on Cumbrian life.

Let off steam in Carlisle
Located next to Carlisle's castle and river, Bitts Park is the city's principal green space and a blissful escape from the traffic-congested ring road. There are lots of free activities, with a children's play area, maze and playing fields, as well as a putting green, crazy golf and tennis courts. Look out for the herb gardens and the sculpture *Towards the Sea* by the Japanese sculptor Hideo Furuta, on the banks of the River Eden.

Explore a typical North Lakes village
For a flavour of a typical north Cumbrian village away from the crowds, it doesn't get much more authentic than Burgh-by-Sands

(burghbysands-parishcouncil. co.uk), five miles west of Carlisle, along the A595 and then B5307. The picture-perfect village lies within an Area of Outstanding Natural Beauty, with views across the Solway Firth. It has history (it's built on the site of the original Hadrian's Wall), nature (curlews and oystercatchers on the marshes), and a local claim to fame: Edward I was killed in a battle with Robert the Bruce here in 1307; a statue in his honour stands on the smart new village green, while the hike down to the Edward I Monument makes for a gentle late-afternoon stroll. The local pub, the Greyhound Inn, could do with a revamp but serves decent pub fare while accommodation at Rosemount Cottage (see page 104), mixes rustic charm and home comforts. Best of all, Burgh is a good place for a tranquil break away from the high-summer frenzy of the national park.

Statue of Edward I,
Burgh-by-Sands
village green.

Discover Ullswater

At 7½ miles long, Ullswater is the second-largest lake in Cumbria and is often described as England's most beautiful lake. It is steeped in myth and legend and sometimes referred to as the 'Dark Lake'. It sits in a location rich in biodiversity with regular sightings of red squirrels, red deer and Barnacle geese. It rests in the shadow of Helvellyn, England's third-highest mountain, which rises at the southern end of the lake.

Ullswater is about five miles southwest of Penrith, with access to the northern head of the lake via Pooley Bridge on the B320. The landscape here is characterized by green rolling hills and flat fields, while the southern hub, Glenridding, off the A592, is ringed by dramatic Lakeland peaks.

During the early 19th century, Wordsworth and his sister Dorothy often came to stay in Ullswater, and it was alongside this very shoreline that, in April 1802, he saw a profusion of daffodils at Gowbarrow Park, inspiring the poem *Daffodils*.

On the shoreline of the southwestern fringe of the lake, Gowbarrow Park is a useful place to break the journey to stretch those legs. From here, it's a short climb (500 m) to Aira Force, one of the most visited waterfalls in the Lake District.

The main attraction for children is a cruise with Ullswater Steamers (see page 93), in business since 1859. Four classic steamers offer pleasure cruises, including on heritage boats dating back to 1877. Services call at Pooley Bridge, Howtown and Glenridding and connect with bus services from Penrith.

The eastern side of the lake is better suited to swimming, although be aware that shoreline shelves can plummet to vast depths. Dotted around the shore are various marinas for boat hire and water sports, as well as fishing. For canoe and kayak hire, see page 90.

Also recommended

Haweswater

This is the highest lake in the Lake District. The eastern end was dammed in 1940 and the Mardale Valley was flooded, submerging the village of Mardale Green. The ruins of the underwater village re-emerge during times of drought.

Aira Force Beck.

Ullswater boathouse.

Penrith

Penrith is the main springboard for visiting the Eden Valley, and with its rough-hewn charm represents a good base to sample life in a working market town in the eastern Lakes. It does feel somewhat stuck in the past, but in an endearing kind of way: think traditional shops, cobbled alleyways and a good range of independent retailers plying their wares. Indeed, many local retailers have campaigned vehemently against plans for a new out-of-town shopping development called Penrith New Squares, the fate of which still appears to be undecided.

Penrith's market charter was granted in the 13th century and the town remains a bustling, commercial centre, radiating from red-brick Market Square. The town also maintains strong links to the regional farming community.

'Old Red Town', as it is known locally (a reference to the town's prevailing sandstone architecture), offers just a handful of visitor attractions per se, but abounds with life and energy. As a base to stock up on provisions, sample some local character and explore the dramatic northern lakes, the beautiful Eden Valley and the rolling Pennine hills, it's hard to beat.

Follow in famous footsteps

- William Wordsworth and his sister Dorothy attended school in the **Tudor house** in St Andrew's Place, Penrith. It was here that he first met Mary Hutchinson, his future wife.

- In November 1745 Bonnie Prince Charlie lodged at the **George Hotel** (see page 106), formerly known as the George and Dragon Inn, on his way south to try to regain the throne for the Stuarts.

- Percy Topliss, known as the 'Monocled Mutineer' was shot dead by police north of Penrith, and is buried in the local cemetery. **Penrith Museum** (see page 88) has a section devoted to his story.

Essential websites

visiteden.co.uk
penrithtowntrails.co.uk
eden.gov.uk

Penrith was the regional capital of Cumbria until 1070.

Get your bearings

Penrith is located off junction 40 of the M6. Ullswater Road leads into town, a 10-minute journey that passes the train station by the proposed Penrith New Squares. The station is on the West Coast Main Line, with connections to Carlisle, Oxenholme (for Kendal) and Lancaster. The best bets for parking are by the New Squares development in the south of town or in the pay-and-display car parks by Morrisons supermarket on Brunswick Road (between the station and town hall).

The helpful staff at the tourist information centre (T01768-867466, visiteden.co.uk, year round Mon-Sat 0930-1730, Sun 1000-1600) can dispense lots of useful information about the town, the Eden Valley and the nearby North Pennines, plus details of attractions across the wider region. The centre even produces special brochures for tots and teens.

On the hunt

Take the kids on a treasure hunt by following one of the official **town trails**, detailed in a leaflet available from the tourist information centre. They can notch up eight blue plaques on the Blue

Let's go to... Penrith

Plaque Trail while learning more about famous people associated with the town, or follow the Millennium Trail, highlighting points of interest and marked with brass plaques in the pavement. The Richard III Trail is an interesting jaunt tracking the town's associations with this king.

Alternatively, head out of town for a gentle one-mile stroll along Fell Lane to follow a wooded path to the summit of **Beacon Hill** (or drive from the centre and park on Beacon Edge before walking up the hill). The **Beacon Tower** was built in 1719 on the spot where fires had traditionally been lit to warn of approaching danger. The views from the top are spectacular, stretching all the way to the Solway Firth and the Lakeland fells.

If you're short of time, head for **Castle Park** for a run around and a quick burst on the swings.

Don't miss

Penrith Castle
english-heritage.org.uk. Easter-Oct 0730-2100, Nov-Easter 0730-1630.
Situated opposite the train station, the castle was first built in the late 14th century with additions by Richard, Duke of Gloucester in the 15th century. After Richard's death at the Battle of Bosworth Field, the castle fell into disrepair and is today a ruin with open access. Kids can climb the weather-beaten ramparts then burn off some energy running round the adjoining Castle Park.

Penrith Museum
T017688-65105, eden.gov.uk/museum. Year round Mon-Sat 0930-1700, Sun 1300-1700. Free.
Located in the tourist information centre, the little museum has local memorabilia, including artefacts celebrating Cumbrian wrestling, and a section on Percy Topliss, 'The Monocled Mutineer', see box page 87.

St Andrew's Church
Behind Market Square.
The churchyard of this 18th-century chapel has two Celtic crosses and four pre-Norman tombstones, known locally as the Giant's Thumb and Giant's Grave. Their mysterious origins are linked variously to a legendary giant and a 10th-century Cumbrian king.

Grab a bite

A reliable option for lunch or dinner is the **Bewick** (Princes St, T01768-864764), a smart café-bistro just north of Crown Square. There's a good choice of mains, including the trademark salad bowls (£7.75), and the kids' menu includes some healthy options for around £3. Check the blackboard for the daily choice of home-made desserts and cakes – favourites include frangipane, baked shortbread and carrot cake.

---

❷ The C2C (Sea to Sea) cycle route passes through Penrith, which has also been designated Cumbria's first Cycling Hub, featuring enhanced infrastructure for cyclists, such as cycle shops, cycling hire and cycle routes.

Also good for a quick bite are **Costas Tapas Bar** (T01768-895550) on Queen Street, the **Magic Bean** (T01768-867474) on Poet's Walk and, for a fish supper, the **Townhead Fish and Chip Shop** (T01768-864988) on Stricklandgate.

If you're self catering, don't miss delicatessen **J&J Graham** (see page 108) and Butchers Guild-approved **Cranstons** (King St, T01768-865667, cranstons.net), a local favourite since 1914. Look out for regional specialities, such as North Cumbrian salt marsh lamb and Tunworth soft cheese. Cranstons has another outlet at the **Cumbrian Food Hall** on Ullswater Road (T01768-868680). There's also a

Market Square, Penrith.

N Arnison & Son, Penrith.

farmers' market in the **Market Square** on the third Tuesday of each month.

Castle Park and the **Coronation Garden** are both good spots for a picnic. Finish off an alfresco lunch with some Penrith fudge and toffee from the **Toffee Shop** (see opposite)

Plan a big day's shopping

One of Penrith's key claims to fame is its abundance of small, independent shops, the likes of which have been edged out of many British high streets by the arrival of chain-shop behemoths. One worth checking out is **The Toy Chest** (Devonshire Arcade, T01768-891237) for soft toys and collectable teddy bears.

But the key exponent of independent retailing is **N Arnison & Sons** (T01768-862078), a museum-piece 'drapers, costumiers and milliners' on Devonshire Street, not unlike Grace Brothers in the popular Seventies TV series *Are You Being Served?* (Google it, youngsters.)

A specialist shops trail is included in the choice of official town trails. Some of the more noteworthy stops include **Eden House of Cakes** (Sandgate, T01768-899225), **Joseph Cowper** pharmacy (King St, T01768-862063) and the **Lion Gallery** (Little Dockray, T01768-867299). Ask at the tourist information centre for the leaflet Penrith Specialist Shops – and get exploring!

You're Penrith born and bred. What are your favourite places around town and how has the town changed?
Penrith is still a nice, old-fashioned market town with lots of privately owned shops. Some of my favourites include Cranstons and The Toy Chest, while N Arnison & Sons is a local legend.

The local authorities have started a £39 million project to build a new, out-of-town shopping centre but it has stalled, so one side of town looks like a bomb site now. I do worry about losing the market-town character of Penrith. It used to thrive on Tuesday market day, once the only day that pubs could stay open all day. But, overall, business is still good.

Why is your shop a bit of a hidden gem in Penrith?
Mrs Furness founded the shop at 33 King Street nearly 100 years ago. I bought the business nearly 30 years ago now but I still use the same recipe and the same ingredients. They have been passed down through the generations.

Neil Boustead, fudge maker by royal appointment, The Toffee Shop, Brunswick Rd, T01768-862008, thetoffeeshop.co.uk.

Action stations

Canoeing & kayaking
Lakeland Boat Hire
Pooley Bridge, T01768-486800,
lakelandboathire.co.uk.
Hire canoes or kayaks for a
water-bound adventure with
older children on Ullswater, see
page 85.

Cycle hire
CycleActive
Brougham, T01768-840400,
cycleactive.co.uk. Bikes £17/day,
tag-a-long or trailer £10/day.
Easy pedalling on quiet lanes
in the Eden Valley, with family
routes of four to six miles. Staff
provide guidance on suitable
routes according to the age of
children and level of fitness.

Fishing
Bessy Beck's Trout Fishery
Newbiggin-on-Lune, T01539-
623303, bessybecktrout.co.uk.
Year round Wed-Sun from 0800,
£3 for 4 hrs' fishing.
Just west of Kirkby Stephen on
the A685 (junction 38 of the
M6), Bessy Beck's is a great place
for youngsters to have a go at
catching their own fish and
learn about the origins of food.
Open to complete novices, it is
suitable for ages two to teens,
with Heron Lake, one of three
lakes, the most popular for
families. Afterwards, the tearoom
has home-made gingerbread;
it also hosts fishing-themed
children's parties.

Penrith Angling Association
T01768-88294,
penrithanglers.co.uk.
The club controls 37 miles of
riverbank, offering some of the
best wild brown trout fly fishing
in the country. Daily and weekly
tickets are available from Charles
R Sykes fishing tackle shop in
Penrith and local post offices. .
Please note that anglers (including
children aged 12-16) must have a
National Fishing Licence.

Foraging & cookery
Augill Little Cooks
South Stainmore, nr Kirkby Stephen,
CA17 4DE, T01768-341937,
stayinacastle.com.
Feb-Oct, £45 child.
Four miles north of Kirkby
Stephen, on the A685, the latest
venture from this award-winning
hotel (see page 106) is a cookery
school aimed at children aged
seven to 14. The day class
(1100-1600) includes collecting
produce from the garden,
preparing lunch then, after a
break to explore the grounds,
making a dish to take home.
All equipment is provided and
the emphasis is on education
and fun. Real skills are acquired
during the day, from filleting fish
to making profiteroles.

Horse riding
Leacett Cottage
Riding Stables
South Whinfell, nr Melkinthorpe,
Penrith, T07939-240214,
leacettridingcentre.co.uk.
Pony trekking for all abilities
from aged two upwards, from
beginners to experienced riders.

Parkfoot Trekking Centre
Pooley Bridge, Ullswater, T017684-
86696, parkfootponytrekking.co.uk.
Escorted pony trekking for
families (minimum age five).

Stonetrail Holidays
Ravenstonedale, CA17 4LL, T01539-
623444, stonetrailholidays.com.
Year round £45/2-hr ride.
The gloriously scenic location
on the Pennine Bridleway in
the Eden Valley fells adds to the
charm of this rustic riding school.
The trail rides are best suited to
experienced riders aged nine
and over, as the terrain can
be demanding. Tuition is also
offered. There's also luxurious,
self-catering accommodation.
Located on the A683, five miles
from the M6 (junction 37).

Multi activities
Rookin House Equestrian &
Activity Centre, Ullswater
T01768-483561, rookinhouse.co.uk.
Archery, Argo Cat off-road
experience, assault course, horse
riding and quad bike treks.

Bike & hike
the North & East Lakes

Hadrian's Wall signpost.

Tourist Information Centre, Carlisle
Old Town Hall, Carlisle, CA3 8JE,
T01228-625600.
Publishes the leaflet *Cycle Carlisle*,
which describes five cycling routes
in and around the city, varying from
12-27 miles.

Arragons Cycle Centre
Penrith, CA11 7LU, T01768-890344,
arragons.com.

Cycle Café
Greystoke Cycle Café, Greystoke, nr
Penrith, CA11 0UT, T01768-483984,
greystokecyclecafe.co.uk.

Pedal Pushers
Sandy Lonning, Brampton, CA8 1RA,
T01697-742387.

Essential
websites
lakedistrictoutdoors.co.uk
hadrians-wall.org.uk
cycle-routes.org/
hadrianscycleway
reivers-guide.co.uk
cyclingcumbria.co.uk

Northern Cumbria offers some of
the best walking and cycling routes
in Britain. Consult local tourist
information centres for sections of
the trails which are particularly suited
to children. The main trails are:

Bike it
• **Hadrian's Cycleway (174 miles)** runs
between Ravenglass and Tynemouth
via Carlisle, passing through Carlisle's
Bitts Park.
• **Reivers Cycle Route (172 miles,
Sustrans route 10)** weaves its way
through the Borders. Starts at Tynemouth
and ends at Whitehaven.

Hike it
• **Hadrian's Wall Path National Trail (84
miles)** follows the course of the Roman
wall between Bowness-on-Solway and
Wallsend at Tynemouth (via Carlisle). The
leg between Birdoswald and Gilsland
(2 miles) is good for families. In summer,
catch the Hadrian's Wall bus back to
Birdoswald to avoid the steep climb
back up the hill.

• **Cumbria Way (77 miles)** is a popular
scenic trail through the heart of the
Lake District that runs from Ulverston
(see page 130) to Carlisle.

• **Cumbria Coastal Way (150 miles)**
follows paths close to the Cumbrian
shoreline.

• **Miller's Way (51 miles)** is a long-
distance trail that opened in 2006 to
mark the 175th anniversary of the
founding of Carr's flour, bread and
biscuit dynasty in Carlisle.

• **East Cumbria Countryside Project**
(eccp.org.uk) produces a series of
Discover Eden booklets, detailing walks
and features of interest along the
River Eden. Pick them up from tourist
information centres.

Walking
Aira
Force

Lake cruises
Ullswater Steamers

Glenridding CA11 0US, T01768-482229, ullswater-steamers.co.uk. Freedom of the Lake Pass £12, £6 child, £29.75 family (includes half-price voucher for the Ravensglass & Eskdale Railway, see page 154). A genteel cruise in three stages (Glenridding Pier House–Howtown Pier–Pooley Bridge Pier House) is a great way to while away a lazy afternoon. The views of England's third-highest mountain, Helvellyn, are amongst the best you will find. Ask about off-season themed cruises, such as the Ghostly Galleon and the Santa and his Happy Elf cruise in December.

Hadrian's Wall

Spanning 73 miles and 2000 years of history, from Bowness-on-Solway to the northeast coast, Hadrian's Wall is the most important monument built by the Romans in Britain. The wall was designated a UNESCO World Heritage site in 1987 and remains the best-known frontier in the entire Roman Empire, an enduring testament to one of the world's greatest civilizations.

With Roman Britain being on the National Curriculum, you can take heart knowing that a visit is both a great family day out away from the national park and hugely educational.

The Emperor Hadrian consolidated the Roman frontier in northern Britain by establishing a man-made border along natural features. In front of the wall spread the civilized world, beyond it lay the barbarians. Merchants had to pay tax and have their carts inspected to enter the Empire; raids and violent skirmishes were common.

Today this off-the-beaten track area of northern Cumbria is a glorious place to soak up a sense of history, explore a vital part of British heritage and marvel at the ingenuity and engineering prowess of the Roman Empire.

March like a Roman
English Heritage manages Hadrian's Wall and brings history to life with a programme of events and family-friendly activities during the school holidays – many are free. Examples include making a Roman helmet and taking part in a Roman drill. More information from English Heritage (T0870-333 1181, english-heritage.org.uk).

Get your bearings

You can launch an invasion of Hadrian's Wall using most means of transport. By car, junction 43 (Carlisle) of the M6 is the access point, with the A69 connecting with the rural B roads.
By following the A69 you can stop off at the Brampton Tourist Information Centre (Market Place, CA8 1RW, T01697-73433. Easter-Oct Mon-Sat 1000-1700) for maps and brochures. Or push on to the Haltwhistle Tourist Information Centre (Northumberland, NE49 0AH, T01434-322002, info@hadrians-wall.org).

Alternatively, the Hadrian's Wall Country Bus (AD 122) runs the full length of the wall from Newcastle to Carlisle, stopping at the main sites, with onward services to Bowness-on-Solway. Some buses have the capacity to carry bicycles and wheelchairs; details are available from local tourist information centres.

Plan a big day out

Birdoswald Roman Fort, Greenhead, 8 miles east of Brampton (signposted from the A69), CA8 7DD, T016977-47602. Apr-Oct daily 1000-1700, £4.80 adult, £2.40 child, under-5s free.
Birdoswald, or Banna as it was known in Roman times, is the main centre of interest for visitors to Hadrian's Wall and a history teacher's dream with its Roman fort, turret and milecastle. (A milecastle is a small rectangular fortification placed at intervals of one Roman mile along major frontiers, like Hadrian's Wall.) The historical exhibition tells

Don't miss

Lanercost Priory

Two miles northeast of Brampton, signposted from the A69 (nr Brampton, CA8 2HQ, T01697-73030, Apr-Sep daily 1000-1700, Oct and Nov Thu-Mon, £3, £1.50 child, under 5s free), is the stunning ruin of a 13th-century Augustinian monastery. It makes for a striking façade on a sunny day. The well-preserved chancel and transepts are buzzing with history. There's a tearoom and gift shop next door to stock up on snacks.

Off the beaten track Hadrian's Wall

the story of the wall from Roman times to the most recent excavations in 1998.

Birdoswald was one of 16 Roman forts built along the wall, its location chosen by Roman planners for its natural vantage point. Legionnaires cleared the forested site in around AD 122, starting its construction with turf and timber and later using limestone and mortar. The Romans ruled the region for over 300 years until around AD 410. At its height, Birdoswald would have accommodated a garrison of over 1000 soldiers drawn from all corners of the Roman Empire.

Pick up the self-guided trail map from the shop and set off to explore, entering the fort by the former West Gate. Follow the route through the granaries and the drill hall, skirting the fort's perimeter, to the panoramic look-out point where a sheer drop falls away to the countryside while buzzards swoop overhead.

The view is dramatic, but more alarming is the knowledge that the fort will eventually collapse into the River Irthing below, as the effects of erosion take hold, a sobering reminder that, like the Roman Empire itself, nothing lasts forever, and Mother Nature always holds the last card.

Check out the hostel

For budget accommodation in atmospheric surroundings, the **YHA Birdoswald** (Gilsland, nr Carlisle, CA6 7DD, T0845-3719551, yha.org.uk, Jul

Activity schedule, Birdoswald Roman Fort, Brampton.

Sponge on a stick

Casting your eye over the soldiers' quarters in the forts along Hadrian's Wall, you can't fail to notice the latrines. You begin to realize how the Romans brought civilization to the far-flung corners of their empire. A channel of gravity-fed running water topped by a stone bench with holes in it provided a communal place to relieve oneself after a hard day suppressing the local populace.

But what are the stone troughs you see in the centre of the room? They would have contained a weak vinegar solution for the tersorium – the sponge tied to a wooden stick that the Romans used instead of toilet paper.

Of course, what the archaeologists disagree on is whether the legionary arrived at the toilet with his tersorium and washed it in the trough, or whether he arrived empty-handed and used one of the tersorium provided in the trough. Either way, no self-respecting Roman legionnaire would be without his sponge on a stick.

For the very best in Roman bathroom design, see Housesteads Roman Fort or Vindolanda Fort; see under Top 10 opposite.

and Aug, £17.95 dorm, £57.95 family) includes entry to Birdoswald fort (see page 95) but not breakfast. The hostel operates only during the summer holidays – it reverts to being an education centre when the schools go back in September. Facilities are top notch: a self-catering kitchen with an Aga, disabled access downstairs and spacious rooms, each with its own toilet and shower. Best of all is the sense of staying on the hallowed earth of history, with some of the original Roman stones cut into the fabric of the building. After all, you are staying within the former Roman fort. Latter-day gladiators will heartily approve.

Find a place to stay

There are plenty of rustic little B&Bs and a handful of hostels across the region, although they tend to cater for walkers following the wall rather than families. More appropriate and worth checking out is **Tantallon House** (Gilsland, nr Carlisle, CA8 7DA,

T01697-747111, hadrians-wall-bed-and-breakfast.co.uk, year round from £70 double), a friendly and homely little guesthouse situated a stone's throw from Birdoswald. Check out the aviary.

Also worth trying are the following:

Bessiestown Farm Country Guesthouse (Longtown, nr Carlisle, CA6 5QP, T01228-577219, bessiestown.co.uk), farmstead B&B and complex of self-catering cottages.

Hesket House (Port Carlisle, CA7 5BU, T01697-351876, heskethouse.com), an 18th-century former steam packet inn.

Newtown Farm B&B (Newtown Irthington, T01697-72768, newtownfarmbedandbreakfast.co.uk) with three-star accommodation on a working farm.

Wallsend Guesthouse (Bowness-on-Solway, T01697-351055, wallsend.net), a traditional B&B in an old rectory.

National Trails also publishes a pamphlet called *Where to Stay for Walkers*. Pick up a copy at the tourist information centre in Carlisle or at other local centres.

Grab a bite

Stock up on Kendal Mint Cake and Mars Bars before setting off on a wall invasion – you'll need the energy. A few recommended places to refuel in the area are:

Café and Farm Shop (Orton Grange, near Carlisle, T 01228-711410, ortongrange.co.uk), a ruddy-cheeked, multi-purpose farm facility with the Orton Grange Café, a farm shop and ice-cream parlour.

Hope and Anchor (Port Carlisle, CA7 5BU, T01697-351460, hopeandanchorinn.com) for no-nonsense pub grub and kids' menu.

Kings Arms (Bowness-on-Solway, CA7 5AF, T01697-351426, kingsarmsbowness.co.uk), a traditional Cumbrian pub for hearty fare with local salmon specials.

Top 10
along the wall

❶ **Birdoswald Roman Fort**, T01697-747602, english-heritage.org.uk.

❷ **Haltwhistle**, T01434-321242, haltwhistle.org.

❸ **Roman Army Museum**, T01697-747485, vindolanda.com.

❹ **Vindolanda Fort**, T01434-344277, vindolanda.com.

❺ **Housesteads Roman Fort**, T01434-344363, nationaltrust.org.uk.

❻ **Chesters Roman Fort**, T01434-681379, english-heritage.org.uk.

❼ **Corbridge**, T01434-652220, thisiscorbridge.co.uk.

❽ **Aydon Castle**, T01434-632450, english-heritage.org.uk.

❾ **Hexham**, T01434-652220, hexhamnet.co.uk.

❿ **Segedunum Roman Fort**, Baths & Museum, T0191-236 9347, twmuseums.org.uk.

Walking along Hadrian's Wall from Birdoswald Roman Fort, Brampton.

Out & about North & East Lakes

Big days out

A World in Miniature Museum

Houghton Hall Garden Centre, Houghton, nr Carlisle, CA6 4JB, T01228-400388, aworldinminiature. com. Year round Mon-Sat 1000-1700, Sun 1030-1630, £3.99 adult, £1.99 child, £10 family.

Located one mile east of Carlisle on the A689, Houghton Hall Garden Centre offers so much more than fertilizer and bulbs. Head through the labyrinthine garden centre, dodge the farm shop and go down the stairs by the gifts section to find a secret world of exquisite miniature models of scenes from around the world.

A private collection open to the public, the exhibits are made to an exacting one-twelfth scale. Look out for the medieval dining hall and the copy of Rembrandt's Gallery.

Next door is a toy shop (with a giant Hornby train set) and the Doll's House

A World in Miniature Museum.

Emporium, selling ready-made and kit-form dolls' houses, plus myriad accessories. Quirky.

Hadrian's Wall

See page 94.

Statesman Rail train services

T0845-310 2458, statesmanrail. com. Returns from £59, £45 child in standard class; return fares with table service in Premier Dining from £139 adult and child – book online for 5% discount on the normal fares. The new, steam-hauled Fellsman service from Statesman Rail is a living-heritage excursion back in time to the golden age of rail travel. It is the first timetabled steam train to operate on the historic Settle to Carlisle line in over 40 years. The company uses a pool of three restored steam engines from the Thirties and period carriages from the Fifties with table seats, panoramic windows and table service in Premier class.

Take a tour

With a 2000-year history of human occupation, Carlisle, the border city and capital of Cumbria, has plenty to interest visitors. Open Book Visitor Guiding (T01228-670578, greatguidedtours.co.uk) runs guided walking tours of the castle, the Citadel or the city centre. It also runs tours focusing on the history, wildlife and geology around Hadrian's Wall. Prices from £2.50 for the one-hour castle tour to £80 for a half-day walking tour along Hadrian's Wall. Call for tailor-made tour prices.

❸ Carlisle is the only English city not recorded in the Doomsday Book, as the city was part of Scotland at the time of the survey in 1086.

Trains run every Wednesday throughout summer. The train picks up passengers from Lancaster and cuts a splendidly scenic, 260-mile swathe along the mountainous Yorkshire-Cumbria frontier. There are easy connections to and from the West Coast Main Line for wider connections.

"Rail is still the best way to see Britain," says Nick Dodson, Chairman of Statesman Rail, which operates the service. "Steam trains smell of nostalgia and the Fellsman harks back to the golden age with its standards of service and dining."

Saved from closure some 20 years ago, the Settle and Carlisle line is now regarded as one of the great train routes in Britain, running northwards and almost parallel to the M6 and West Coast Main Line route to Scotland. It's a testament to the Victorian engineering that not only built a network around Britain, but also introduced railways to India, Africa and South America.

Track construction started in 1869 with a workforce of 6000 men – over 200 went on to lose their lives on the job. The passenger service started running in 1876 after a total investment of £3.5 million to launch the route. The combination of challenging climatic conditions, steep gradients and complex engineering of the 21 stone-built viaducts, 14 tunnels and numerous bridges fostered a reputation as a one-off ride. It is immortalized in the 1955 short film, *Snowdrift at Bleath Gill,* held by the British Transport Film archive. More information from settlecarlisle.co.uk.

Tullie House

Carlisle, CA3 8TP, T01228-618718, tulliehouse.co.uk. Year round Mon-Sat from 1000, Sun from 1200, £5.20 adults, children free.
This is a good place to swot up on Roman history before a trip to Hadrian's Wall (see page 94). Enquiring minds should head

---

❷ The first free-standing letterbox on mainland Britain was installed on Botchergate, Carlisle in 1853.

Visit Upfront Gallery & Puppet Theatre

Why? Roll up! Roll up! These converted 17th-century farm buildings are home to a vegetarian café, an art gallery and – he's behind you! – a puppet theatre. There's a changing programme of shows suitable for ages four upwards, plus the 1530 show is normally followed by a 'Meet the Puppets' session. If you loved the show, you can even buy your own puppet in the shop afterwards. The café owners are also the puppeteers and don't like being interrupted during a performance. But that's puppeteers for you: highly strung. Boom, boom!

Where? Nr Hutton-in-the-Forest, Unthank, Penrith, CA11 9TG, T01768-484538, up-front.com. Three miles along the B5305 from the M6 (junction 41).

How? End of Jan to mid-Dec Tue-Sun 1030-1630, plus bank holiday Mondays. £6 for puppet show, around £7 mains in the vegetarian café.

Walby Farm Park, near Carlisle.

upstairs to the Border Galleries for an explanation of Carlisle's development as a rail hub and its role in the story of Roman Britain. The kids can play at soldiers by scaling a life-sized section of Hadrian's Wall. There are regular events for children, especially during school holidays. The gift shop has books and games, while the restaurant is stocked with high chairs and family-favourite food. Take

Hit or miss?

High Head Sculpture Valley
High Head Farm, Ivegill,
CA4 0PJ, T01697-473552,
highheadsculpturevalley.co.uk.
Year round Thu-Tue 1030-1630,
£2.50 adult, £1.50 child, under-
6s free.

Could an obscure sculpture trail on the spare acres of a working dairy farm really grab the attention of children? Well, actually, yes. High Head Farm, found by following signs from the M6 (junction 41) for Wigton (B5305), is a hidden gem in the countryside outside Carlisle with a one-mile circular walk around the farm, taking in the work of local artists en route. The location is the key attraction here with a gentle woodland saunter, often accompanied by the farm's friendly canines, making for an idyllic way to stretch the legs after a couple of hours on the M6. A tearoom, kids' clothes shop and a small adventure playground (suitable up to nine years) complete the picture.
Ahh, peace…

your tray out into the adjoining garden for an impromptu picnic – but beware of the birds.

Walby Farm Park

Crosby-on-Eden, nr Carlisle, CA6 4QL, T01228-573056, walbyfarmpark. co.uk. Year round daily 1000-1800, £5.95 adult, £5.45 child, £21 family, under-1s free.

Located off the A689 (follow signs for Brampton) four miles east of Carlisle and the M6 (junction 44), this superb farm park was voted Cumbria Tourism's Large Visitor Attraction of the Year 2009. You can see why. It's an all-weather facility with indoor and outdoor attractions for all ages and has the homely atmosphere of a working farm. For rainy days, the indoor play centre has giant slides and the Curly Tails Café with pick 'n' mix lunch boxes (£3.50 for four items).

Outside, the animal paddocks have pygmy goats, alpacas and sheep, with lots of background information provided. It also has a petting area and a huge play area with views across the Pennines and the Lakes.

For the best fun, head for the tractor tower, converted from an old slurry tank, and burn it up, Jeremy Clarkson-style, on a mini-tractor.

❷ Pigs sleep for 13 hours per day according to the animal experts at Walby Farm Park.

Rain check

Cinemas
• **Lonsdale Allhambra**, Penrith, T01768-862400, lonsdalecitycinemas.co.uk.
• **Vue Cinema**, Carlisle, T01228-819988, myvue.com.

Indoor play & amusements
• **Pirates of Penrith**, Gilwily Industrial Estate, Penrith, T01768-840572.
• **The Sands Centre**, Carlisle, T01228-625222, thesandscentre.co.uk.

Indoor swimming pools
• **Penrith Leisure Centre & Climbing Wall**, Penrith, T01768-863450, leisure-centre.com.

• **The Pools**, Carlisle, T01228-625777, carlisleleisure.com.

Museums
• **Brougham Castle**, Penrith, T01768-862488, english-heritage.org.uk.
• **Brougham Hall**, Penrith, T017688-68184, broughamhall.co.uk.

Karting, bowling, Laser Quest
• **AMF Bowling**, Carlisle, T0844-826 3013, amfbowling.co.uk.
• **Carlisle Indoor Karting**, Newtown Industrial Estate, Carlisle, T01228-510061, carlisleindoorkarting.co.uk.
• **Laserquest**, Carlisle, T01228-511155, lquk.com.

Don't miss Tebay Motorway Services

Question: when is a motorway service station not a motorway service station?
Answer: when it's Tebay.

Yes, we know. A service station at junction 38 of the M6 doesn't sound like a top Cumbrian tourist attraction, but family-owned Tebay is one of only two independent service stations in the UK (the other is in Scotland) and a far cry from your common-or-garden Welcome Break. Hence the reason why it's hugely popular and a must-stop staging post for many people venturing into the wide-open spaces of northern Cumbria.

In fact, the latest figures show that the north and south stations each attract some 1.6 million visitors a year. Southbound has been recently refurbished with northbound to follow. Egon Ronay declared Tebay the best services in England in 2000 and the awards have flowed ever since.

The sprawling site comprises a mid-range hotel (northbound), the decidedly upmarket and local produce-championing Westmorland Farm Shops (both sides) and dual service stations.

The latter is what really sets Tebay apart. The open-plan **Southbound Café** is particularly family- friendly with a flora and fauna-themed play zone and a kids' garden. There are separate family bathrooms with low sinks, changing mats and low toilets, while the Kids' Corner of the restaurant

has a low-level display and offers lunchboxes for a pick 'n' mix-style healthy lunch. Price wise, it offers better value than the typical motorway service station (budget £8.50 for the roast of the day, £3.50 for a kids' set meal), for the quality is far superior, with home-made dishes using local produce. The beef and lamb, for example, comes from Dunning's Farm, next to the services.

> ❷ The most popular cheese at the Westmorland Farm Shops is Cumberland Farmhouse from the Thornby Moor Dairy. The shops sell over 1500 kg per year.

On a sunny day, grab a sausage sandwich from the outdoor kiosk, perch on a stone seat in the grounds and simply take in the views across the Cumbrian fells. There's even a dog walk for pooches needing a break from cramped cars.

After lunch, while the kids are romping through the play zone, parents can peruse the **Westmorland Farm Shop**, making a beeline for the butcher's counter, which has venison burgers (£1.05 each) and farm-reared pork (£7.99 per kg) amongst other goodies. In fact many of the people stopping by – Tebay can get extremely busy – are locals stocking up on fresh produce. The shop has the usual maps and obscure compilation CDs, but also lots of colouring books and toys to make the journey fly. There's free Wi-Fi too.

The family behind Tebay also own and run the **Rheged Centre** (Penrith, T01768-868000, rheged.com, daily 1000-1730), further north on the M6 (junction 40), which has shops and cafés specializing in local produce, a soft play area, giant cinema screen and a rolling programme of exhibitions on Cumbria (see page 84).

Again, it's a family-friendly option, making a great break to a long journey or a good place to duck into during a heavy downpour. The outdoor shop has a good range of gear for tackling the fells and the deli is fantastically well stocked, but the main draw is the huge programme of activities for kids during the school holidays, ranging from a teddy bears' picnic to a GPS treasure trail. There's free entry and free parking, but budget on paying around £6 per child to join activities.

We've seen the future of motorway services and Little Chef it ain't. And if you don't believe us, take Stuart Maconie's word for it:

"Tebay Services off the M6 is talked of in hushed tones by middle-class drivers from Middle England making the trip north. Not only is the scenery stunning … but this is the Tuscany, the Waitrose, the Keira Knightley of service stations."

Stuart Maconie, *Adventures on the High Teas*, Ebury Press, 2009.

Essential information

Tebay Motorway Services, Orton, nr Penrith, CA10 3SB, T01539-624511, westmorland.com. Year round 24 hrs.

Sleeping North & East Lakes

Pick of the pitches

Lowther Holiday Park

Eamont Bridge, nr Penrith, T01768-863631, lowther-holidaypark.co.uk. Mar-Nov from £22.50/night, including 6 people, awning, electric hook-up and 2 dogs.

◐ ◑ ◒ ◓ ◔ ◕ ◖

Listed by *Practical Caravan* magazine as one of Britain's 'Top 100 family parks', Lowther is set in 50 acres of natural woodland on the banks of the River Lowther. From the M6 (junction 40), take the A66 towards Scotch Corner for one mile and then the A6 south towards Shap for one mile. The park is just after the village of Eamont Bridge. It caters for touring caravans, camper vans and tents, with a good range of facilities, including four children's areas scattered around the site. The owners arrange themed weekends throughout the year, including a kids' sports weekend in May and a treasure hunt in October, with prices starting from £35 for the weekend, including awning, electricity, up to six occupants and one car.

Ullswater Caravan, Camping and Marine Park

Watermillock, nr Penrith, CA11 0LR, T01768-486666, uccmp.co.uk. Mar-Nov, from £17/night per pitch, from £260/week chalets.

◐ ◑ ◒ ◓ ◔ ◕ ◖ ◗

A friendly, family-run site with 13 acres of rolling green pasture for caravans, campers and long-hire static chalets. From the M6 (junction 40) take the A592 signposted Windermere and Patterdale. The on-site family facilities include a children's playground and a games room with TV. Rather handily, the Fairfield Marina, on the banks of Ullswater, is a private lakeside facility just one mile from the site, so there are no excuses not to try some watersports as part of your visit.

Also recommended
Knotts Hill

Howtown, nr Penrith, CA10 2NA, T01768-486309, knottshill.co.uk.

Park Foot Camping & Caravanning Park

Pooley Bridge, nr Penrith, CA10 2NA, T01768-486309, parkfootullswater.co.uk.

Waterside House Campsite

Pooley Bridge, nr Penrith, CA10 2NA, T01768-486332, watersidefarm-campsite.co.uk.

Best of the rest

Hall Hills

Dalston, nr Carlisle, CA5 7AN, T01697-476779, hallhills.co.uk. From £595/week (sleeps 4). Picking up the top gong for Self-Catering Holiday of the Year in both the Cumbria Tourism Awards and the England's Northwest Tourism Awards 2009, Hall Hills' cluster of 17th-century barns have been lovingly converted into upscale holiday accommodation. The properties are situated near the village of Dalston; from the M6 (junction 42) follow the A6 and B5299 heading southwest of Carlisle. Each of the four self-catering properties has its own style and character, with plenty of exposed beams, solid oak floors and a private patio. A complimentary hamper of Cumbrian produce welcomes every arrival.

Rosemount Cottage B&B

Burgh-by-Sands, CA5 8AN, T01228-576440, rosemountcottage.co.uk. From £56/double B&B, from £295/week cottage (sleeps 6). Five miles northwest of Carlisle off the B5307, Rosemount Cottage makes for a great escape away from the crowds. The charming 18th-century cottage offers B&B with comfy rooms, a library-like lounge and a big breakfast served at the kitchen table. For families, the self-catering cottage may be a more practical option: it has a large kitchen and private space away from the main house.

YHA Bridge Lane

Carlisle, T0870-770 5752, yha.org.uk. Jul and Aug only, £22/room, £120/apartment. These simple rooms in a converted brewery revert to being student accommodation come September. But in high

Enchanted forest

Center Parcs Whinfell Forest
Whinfell, nr Penrith, CA10 2DW, T0844-826 6266, centerparcs.co.uk/
villages/whinfell. Year round from £239 (off peak), £519 (peak) short
break for a 2-bedroom villa (sleeps 4). Center Parcs Whinfell Forest is
located on the A66 4 miles southeast of Penrith; from the M6 (junction
40), follow the A66 east toward Brough.

Let's face it: Center Parcs is not everyone's cup of tea. But it does what it does
very well, and happy, busy kids make for a stress-free holiday. So, if you put
your preconceptions aside, what does the Whinfell Forest site actually offer?

It's a 400-acre woodland site, best tackled by bicycle (for hire at £32 adult,
£18 child), with enough nooks and crannies to escape the crowds – even in
the fully booked peak season. It has a nice, close-to-nature feel with lots of
Norway Spruce trees and a community of red squirrels.

There are many activities on offer, but they're not always cheap. While the
Subtropical Swimming Paradise is free to all guests, all other activities are
charged as extra. For example, budget £8 per child for a 45-minute Messy
Play session (ages 18 months to three years) and £6 for a 45-minute Animal
Allsorts Safari (three to seven years).

Some of the best facilities on the site are the aerial confidence courses
with abseiling, zip wire and high ropes, a great way for children to try new
things in a safe environment. Budget £21 per two-hour session; under-eights
must be accompanied by an adult.

The site has lots of retail and restaurant concessions to suit all tastes. The
Indian restaurant Rajinda Pradesh, for example, offers as good a curry as any
downtown curry house, while slick service strikes the right balance between
family friendly and fine dining.

Finally, for some quality time away from the kids, parents can book
babysitting (£8.50/hour, minimum three hours) and head to the bar for a
well-deserved cold one. (Prices correct at time of going to press.)

summer the YHA takes over and does a roaring trade in walkers and cyclists hitting the trails. Rooms come in blocks of seven with a communal kitchen and bathroom. For more space, rent an apartment with kitchenette.

Also recommended
Bank House
Penrith, T01768-868714, bankhousepenrith.co.uk.

Hornby Hall
Broughton, nr Penrith, CA10 2AR, T01768-891114, hornbyhall.co.uk.

Lovelady Shield
Alston, CA9 3LF, T01434-381203, lovelady.co.uk.

Number Thirty One
Carlisle, T01228-597080, number31.co.uk.

Tufton Arms
Appleby, CA16 6XA, T01768-351593, tuftonarmshotel.co.uk.

Willowford Farm
Gilsland, CA8 7AA, T01697-747962, willowford.co.uk.

Cool & quirky

Shacklabank Farm
Firbank, nr Sedbergh, LA10 5EL, T01539-620134, shacklabank.co.uk. Doubles from £60/night B&B, gypsy caravan from £300/week.
Rural Shacklabank is a working farm offering a range of walking holidays and farm experiences

that give children a chance to sample farm life first-hand. It's an intimate, pitch-in experience led by walking guide Alison O'Neill. After a day out exploring in the dramatic Howgill landscapes, families can return to the farm for a home-cooked feast of traditional comfort food, then retire to their cosy caravan to dream sweetly under the patchwork quilt.

Splashing out

Augill Castle
South Stainmore, nr Kirkby Stephen, CA17 4DE, T01768-341937, stayinacastle.com.
Year round £160/doubles B&B, £240 family, plus £15 child sharing.
If you're splashing out, then there are few places making bigger waves in Cumbria. A fairytale setting in a restored hunting lodge, award-winning Augill remains a family home and a defiantly family-friendly place to stay in style. The music

Gardens, Augill Castle.

room is full of DVDs and toys, while adults can head for the drawing room with its adjoining honesty bar. The rooms are contemporary but unfussy, with quieter rooms in a side annexe. Both dinner (£35 weekend, £20 midweek, £5 kids) and breakfast are served *en famille* around a large dining table, which can make for a few awkward silences when your toddlers play up. Still, overall, it's a real experience – as is the kids' cookery school, see Augill Little Cooks, page 90.

George Hotel
Penrith, CA11 7SU, T01768-862696, lakedistricthotels.net/georgehotel.
From £59/room plus £10 child sharing (under-12s).
This venerable old hotel right at the heart of Penrith's Market Square is showing its age a bit, but it offers a broad range of family-friendly facilities, including baby baths, high chairs and special menus, and the rooms are well appointed. The management runs some good promotional offers in the low season – call for details.

Also recommended
Inn on the Lake
Ullswater, nr Glenridding, CA11 0PE, T0800-840 1245, lakedistricthotels. net//innonthelake.

The Weary
Castle Carrock, nr Carlisle, CA8 9LU, T01228-670230, theweary.com.
Stylish restaurant with rooms.

The George Hotel.

Local goodies

Abbott Lodge Jersey Ice Cream

Clifton, nr Penrith, CA10 2HD, T01931-712720, abbottlodgejerseyicecream.co.uk. Easter-Oct daily 1100-1700, Nov-Mar closed Mon and Fri, except bank holidays.

Four miles south of Penrith on the A6, Abbott Lodge is a working dairy farm producing ice cream from the milk of Jersey cows, with some 30-odd delicious flavours to choose from every day. A tearoom and play areas (both outdoor and indoor) complete the picture.

Cranstons Cumbrian Food Hall

Penrith, T01768-868680, cranstons. net. Year round Mon-Sat 0800-1800. An iconic coil of coarsely-chopped pork, black pepper, herbs and spices, the traditional Cumberland sausage is not only delicious, but it doesn't roll off your barbecue like lesser bangers. Local butchers all have their own closely guarded recipes, but Cranstons' recipe

Market days

Penrith Farmers' Market, Market Square, third Tuesday.

Penrith Market, Great Dockray, Penrith, every Tuesday.

Skirsgill Market, Auction Mart, Penrith, every Saturday.

Store room, Watermill, Little Salkeld.

is one of the very best. You can also buy excellent burgers, bacon and pies here, along with a range of other local produce.

Ivinson's Farm Shop

Wetheriggs Farm, Clifton Dykes, nr Penrith, CA10 2DH, T01768-866979, ivinsonsfarmshop.co.uk. Summer Tue-Sun 1000-1700, winter Wed–Sun 1100-1600, Fri and Sat evenings for pre-booked meals only.

Wetheriggs Farm, run by the Ivinson family for generations, recently opened a farm shop selling their own farm-reared lamb and locally sourced beef, sausages and bacon, plus farm-prepared pies, casseroles, quiches, preserves and cakes. There is a tearoom and gift shop, while children can feed the pet ducks, or spot the alpacas and rare breed sheep.

J&J Graham

Market Square, Penrith, CA11 7BS, T01768-862281, jjgraham.co.uk. Year round Mon-Sat 0900-1700. If there's one place in the Lakes you can turn your children into budding foodies, then this is it. Established in 1793, this

treasure-trove delicatessen has enough to get the gastric juices flowing for both adults and kids – think scrummy cakes, tasty pies and yummy chocolates. The take-away wooden boxes of local goodies, such as an Eden Box of meats, cheeses and chutneys for £72.50, make for perfect presents. And nothing beats buying a picnic of goodies from the deli and enjoying them in the Market Square. Come hungry, really hungry.

Watermill

Little Salkeld, nr Penrith, CA10 1NN, T01768-881523, organicmill.co.uk. Eccentric and remote, the Watermill is worth grappling with your Sat Nav to locate. It's a true green escape with the shop selling organic flour milled by the 18th-century waterwheels and the tearoom offering one of the most perfect picture-postcard views in Britain over a plate of vegetarian food (mains around £7.95). Ask about the children's workshop programme, for kids aged five and over, or catch one of the mill tours (£8 family) to soak up the history. It's located six miles northeast of Penrith off the B6412 – look out for signs for the nearby stone circle, Long Meg and Her Daughters.

❷ Long Meg and Her Daughters is the third-largest prehistoric stone circle in England. A curse awaits anyone meddling with the stones, according to ancient folklore.

Also recommended

Carleton Farm Shop

Carleton, nr Penrith, CA11 8RQ, T01768-210027. Year round Mon-Sat 0900-1730, Sun 1000-1600.

Farm Shop, High Head Sculpture Valley

Ivegill, nr Carlisle, CA4 0PJ, T01697-473552, highheadsculpturevalley.co.uk.

Greystone House Tearoom and Farm Shop

Stainton, nr Penrith, T01768-866952. Year round daily 1000-1730. Go during lambing season to see lambs being born.

Quick & simple

Fellbites Café

Glenridding, Ullswater, T017684-82781, fellbites.co.uk. Just what you need after a long family walk, Fellbites has an excellent evening menu, with a two-course meal, such as lamb shank and sticky toffee pudding, costing around £17.50. Lunch snacks and a children's menu are also available.

John Watts & Son Victorian Coffee Shop

Carlisle, T01228-521545, victoriancoffeeshop.co.uk. This historic coffee shop was established in 1865 "to ensure the smell of fresh-roasted coffee continues to drift through the streets of Carlisle." And we salute them for that. Grab a pavement table and watch the world go by over a fair-trade coffee or an exotic-flavoured tea plus simple snacks. It's worth the trip down creaky stairs to the bathroom to check out the ad hoc museum in the basement.

No 15

Penrith, CA11 8HN, T01768-867453. Daily 0900-1700. Penrith's top spot for a caffeine fix is a cool café-gallery with arty photography exhibits and an artily crafted cappuccino. The all-day menu takes in breakfasts and lunches (around £8), a kids' menu (£3.50) and Wi-Fi access (£2). A nice, laid-back enclave.

Queen's Head Inn

Tirril, nr Penrith, CA10 2JF, T01768-863219, queensheadinn.co.uk. A couple of miles southwest of Penrith on the B5320, the Queen's is a country pub with Wii games for kids in the back bar, a lovely sun terrace and some hearty, no-nonsense pub grub (mains around £8.95, kids' menu £4.95). Best of all, it hosts each August the renowned Cumbrian Beer and Sausage Festival with free entry. Aran sweaters not compulsory.

Queen's Head Inn, Tirril.

Posh nosh

Yanwath Gate Inn

Yanwath, nr Penrith CA10 2LF, T01768-862386, yanwathgate.com. Two miles southwest of Penrith on the B5320, the Yanwath Gate Inn was one of Britain's first gastropubs. The Yanwath is nowadays a relaxed country pub with a serious foodie pedigree. Think great local produce imaginatively prepared, plus tasty local cheeses and ales. Lunch lends itself better to families, with mains around £11.

Also recommended

Grants of Castlegate

Penrith, T01768-835444.

Number 10

Carlisle, T01228-524183.

Sharrow Bay

Ullswater, T01768-486301, sharrowbay.co.uk. A Michelin-starred restaurant that claims to be the original home of sticky toffee pudding.

Contents

South Lakes

The steam train,
South Lakes Wild
Animal Park.

You must

1 Hit top gear to the all-new Lakeland Motor Museum.

2 Split your sides at the Laurel & Hardy Museum in Ulverston.

3 Explore remote Low Furness Peninsula on foot, by bicycle or car.

4 Visit the South Lakes Wild Animal Park in Dalton-in-Furness.

5 Raise a glass with the King of Piel on an island.

6 Enjoy a Brief Encounter at the Carnforth Station and Visitor Centre.

7 Linger over lunch in the garden at Gillam's, Ulverston, or tuck into afternoon tea at Hazelmere Café, Grange-over-Sands.

8 Sprinkle salt and vinegar on Cumbria's best chip supper at the Arnside Chip Shop.

9 Explore picture-postcard Cartmel.

10 Stock up on the finest local produce at Holker Food Hall.

Signpost, Cartmel.

This region offers many of the classic delights of a traditional family holiday such as nature walks along coastal paths and boardwalks, woodland bike rides and beach cricket. But it also has the picture-postcard village of Cartmel, the nation's best sticky toffee pudding, and South Lakes Wild Animal Park, a great option for a special day out.

From junction 36 of the M6, the A590 leads away from Lancashire into the rural heart of southern Cumbria, much of which lies outside the boundaries of the Lake District National Park. The place names are less familiar and the roads increasingly empty the further west you head, but the scenery of rolling fells and towering peaks is a reminder that the classic destinations of Coniston, Ambleside and Windermere are still close at hand. And that means you can find cheaper accommodation while still being within easy reach of the action.

The traditional hub for visitors to the South Lakes is **Grange-over-Sands**, an elegant Edwardian resort with a fine line in afternoon teas and a good place for genteel mooching. It feels slightly lost in time, a place that harks back to the Britain of the 1950s, although some places around the town are beginning to move with the times.

For families, an alternative base would be **Ulverston**, a bustling little market town with decent infrastructure for visitors and a great story to tell in connection with its most famous son, the comic actor Stan Laurel, the thin half of Laurel and Hardy. Otherwise, head into the rural heart of southern Cumbria and seek out the tiny village of **Cartmel**, a place so pretty it looks like it has been created for a magazine spread. In fact, it has a rich history, and also has some of the best places to eat in the South Lakes.

Speaking of which, good food is a key ingredient in the appeal of the South. While the region may be missing the range of accommodation available in the other parts of the Lake District, and, with the notable exception of the **South Lakes Animal Park**, lack the big-hitting attractions of the Central Lakes, the South is a superb place to stock up on local produce. From farm shops to a Michelin-starred restaurant via a world-beating pudding, this is one region where you will never go hungry.

But, most of all, the South is about getting back to nature – whether pitching your tent on **Piel Island** or watching the wildlife on the coastal path route around the **Low Furness Peninsula**, the best thing about the South is escaping the crowds, breathing in lungfuls of sea and country air and reconnecting with the natural environment.

A return maybe to the concept of the traditional family holiday of yesteryear, albeit with great local food and comfortable accommodation.

Out & about South Lakes

Play in an ace park

Barrow Park in Barrow-in-Furness is regularly voted one of the best parks in Northwest England and has been awarded a Green Flag for its facilities. An Edwardian gem, it boasts landscaped grounds, a pavilion, a glasshouse and ornamental flowerbeds. More importantly, kids will be won over by the miniature railway, putting green, skate park and play areas, including the first i.play interactive play equipment to be installed in Britain, mixing conventional playground equipment with high-tech electronics, encouraging children to be more active. More details of the i.play system from intelligentplay.co.uk.

Join Ulverston's Lantern Procession

In September Ulverston holds its annual Lantern Procession, which unites the whole town in a colourful parade. Time your visit well and you could join in the fun. At other times of the year the Lanternhouse (T01229-581127, lanternhouse.org), the contemporary arts centre that organizes the Lantern Procession, holds children's workshops in the creative arts.

Eat ice cream in an ancient monument

Cartmel is one of the prettiest villages in the South Lakes and its 12th-century priory is an ecclesiastical gem. The priory was the heart of the community until it was largely destroyed on the orders of Henry VIII during the Dissolution of the Monasteries, but an appeal by villagers to keep the church as a place of worship for the parish was granted, thus saving the church (and the gatehouse) for posterity. A stroll around the priory reveals a fine stained-glass east window, filtering shards of daylight across the

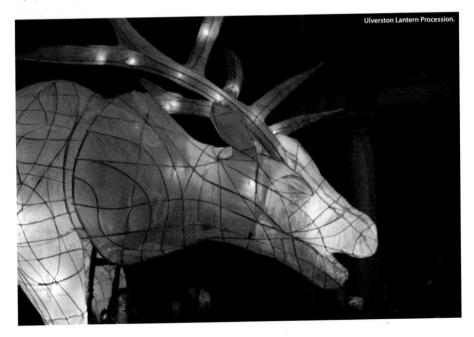

Ulverston Lantern Procession.

The Devil's Bridge over the River Lune near Kirkby Lonsdale.

ancient tombs and rough-hewn stone pillars. In the tranquil churchyard, take a moment to gaze up at the belfry, then reward the kids with a cone of English Lakes Luxury Ice Cream from the priory shop – the Kendal Mint Choc Chip is particularly good, though the kids might prefer Death by Chocolate, Cookies or one of their wackier flavours.

Admire a famous view
One of England's most acclaimed views is Ruskin's View, signposted from the churchyard in Kirkby Lonsdale, just north of the A65. Most visitors to the Lake District miss it, as they hurtle towards the popular Central Lakes, but those taking the detour east will find the roads clearer this side of the M6. The view of the River Lune was painted by Turner and described by Ruskin as 'one of the loveliest in England'; more on the village from kirkbylonsdale.co.uk.

Discover Sunday morning at church

The South Lakes are home to some of the most attractive village churches in Cumbria, and a stroll through the churchyard is a great way for kids to connect to local history. Three of the best churches to explore are:

St Mary's and St Michael's Church, Urswick
The ancient ceremony of rush bearing is celebrated here on the nearest Sunday to St Michael's Day (29 September). Rushes from the nearby tarn are carried in procession through the village and then strewn on the church floor during a special service. The tradition, one shared with several other churches in the area, recalls the time when the church had earth floors. Notable features inside the church include a three-decker Georgian pulpit, some fine woodcarvings and a section of an Anglian cross (the Tunwinni stone), which has a runic inscription.

St Cuthbert's Church, Aldingham
Overlooking Morecambe Bay, this ancient church is thought to occupy a monastic site where the monks of Lindisfarne rested the body of St Cuthbert when fleeing from Viking raiders around AD 875. See if the kids can spot a small hole in the wall behind the altar; it was used to give communion to lepers so that they didn't have to enter the church.

St Michael's and Holy Angels Church, Pennington
The location of this church within a circular churchyard on a prominent knoll suggests this was a site of ancient worship. In 1926, a pagan Sheela-Na-Gig (an engraved image of Freya, the goddess of fertility) was discovered in the eastern wall (it's now on display in Kendal Museum).

Children can let off steam in Promenade Gardens, Grange-over-Sands, overlooking Morecambe Bay.

Explore Grange's town gardens

Ornamental Gardens
The park's splendid centrepiece is a duck pond with a colourful array of ducks and geese from all over the world.

Park Road Gardens
In summer, brass band concerts are regularly held in the park's restored Victorian bandstand.

Promenade Gardens
The promenade walk, fringed by tropical palms and ornamental shrubs, commands fine views of the marshes of Morecambe Bay.

Step back in time

If you sometimes wish life was more like an episode of the TV series *Heartbeat* – the gentle drama set in a cosy corner of Yorkshire in the 1960s – then you'll love spending a weekend in Grange-over-Sands. Grange became a popular seaside resort once the Furness Railway arrived in the late 1850s. Its growing reputation as a fashionable 'riviera' soon attracted wealthy businessmen from Lancashire and Yorkshire, who built many of the graceful homes and hotels in the town. The promenade came later in 1902, providing easy access to the sandy beach. The clean, salty air was believed to be of benefit to tuberculosis sufferers and, in 1891, one of the

first sanatoriums in the British Isles was established at nearby Meathop.

Grange retains much of its Edwardian elegance, with shopping arcades and a seafront promenade. The building of the railway and viaducts led to the silting up of the estuary and changes in the currents, so nowadays the promenade dips its toes into saltmarsh rather than sea water.

There's no scope these days for paddling or rock pooling, but Grange is still a great place to stretch your legs after a long car journey, with a traffic-free promenade and flower-filled public gardens with duck ponds and brass band concerts all summer long.

Seek out the wildlife

The South Lakes is a great place to get back to nature, with a more remote, off-the-beaten-track feel than the Lake District National Park. One of the best places to explore the wild side is the **Hodbarrow Nature Reserve**, a lagoon salvaged from a former industrial site behind the Netherwood Hotel in central Grange. An RSPB site, it is home to a wide variety of bird species, and a haven for birdwatchers; you may even spot a Natterjack toad leaping from lily pad to lily pad.

Sea Wood on Low Furness Peninsula (see page 119) is an ancient woodland that once belonged to Lady Jane Grey (Queen of England for nine days before her execution in 1554). In spring, the woodland floor is carpeted in bluebells, wild garlic, dog's mercury and other flowers. A network of paths radiate through the wood for wildlife-spotting strolls.

Essential
websites

cumbriawildlifetrust.org.uk
naturalengland.co.uk
woodlandtrust.org.uk

❸ The last wolf in England was supposedly killed at Humphrey Head in the 14th century.

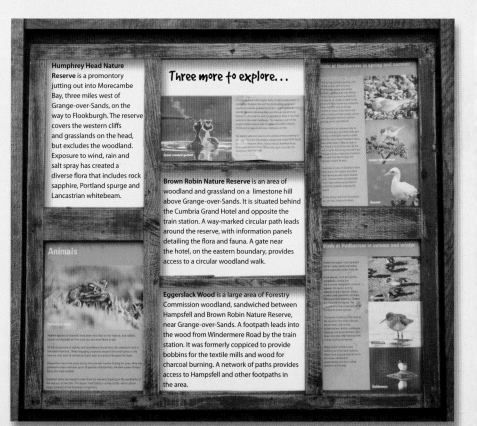

Humphrey Head Nature Reserve is a promontory jutting out into Morecambe Bay, three miles west of Grange-over-Sands, on the way to Flookburgh. The reserve covers the western cliffs and grasslands on the head, but excludes the woodland. Exposure to wind, rain and salt spray has created a diverse flora that includes rock sapphire, Portland spurge and Lancastrian whitebeam.

Animals

Three more to explore...

Brown Robin Nature Reserve is an area of woodland and grassland on a limestone hill above Grange-over-Sands. It is situated behind the Cumbria Grand Hotel and opposite the train station. A way-marked circular path leads around the reserve, with information panels detailing the flora and fauna. A gate near the hotel, on the eastern boundary, provides access to a circular woodland walk.

Eggerslack Wood is a large area of Forestry Commission woodland, sandwiched between Hampsfell and Brown Robin Nature Reserve, near Grange-over-Sands. A footpath leads into the wood from Windermere Road by the train station. It was formerly coppiced to provide bobbins for the textile mills and wood for charcoal burning. A network of paths provides access to Hampsfell and other footpaths in the area.

Low Furness Peninsula

South of Ulverston is the Low Furness Peninsula, an oasis of rural calm compared to the full-on tourism of the national park, especially in high season. With unspoilt villages, quiet footpaths and bridleways, it is ideal for exploring on foot or by bicycle. Alternatively fly a kite on Walney Island, paddle in the sea at Bardsea, or visit South Lakes Wild Animal Park, the South Lakes' star attraction, see page 126.

For families, exploring the peninsula is very much about getting close to nature and savouring the sea air. But not all of the coast is suitable for walking, paddling and exploring. On the coast road (A5087) southwest from Ulverston, Bardsea is the most popular spot for a family day out. It offers safe paddling on a shingle and sand beach and has a cute café for ice creams. Further along, Baycliff beach has good rock pools to explore but fewer facilities. The beach at Aldingham marks the end of the safe stretch – beyond here, most of the coves are closed off by a sea wall.

Get your bearings

The Low Furness Peninsula is Cumbria's most southerly tip, a rural expanse between Ulverston and Barrow-in-Furness. From the M6 (junction 36), follow the A590 into Ulverston. From here, the A590 continues southwest to Barrow-in-Furness, while the A5087 skirts the coastline to take the slow road, offering great views of the Fylde Coast, Morecambe and Blackpool.

The nearest train station is at Ulverston on the Furness Line, with connections to the West Coast Main Line at Carnforth. There are tourist information centres in Ulverston (T01229-587120, southlakeland.gov.uk/tourism) and Barrow-in-Furness (T01229-876505).

Follow the trail

If your children like walks, why not sample a short stretch of the 45-mile **Cumbria Coastal Way**? The five-mile section from Bardsea to Roosebeck Head takes in coastal views and wildlife. The route is summarized in the leaflet *The Cumbria Coastal Way* from the tourist information centre in Ulverston, where you can also buy a tide table (also see page 123 for safety tips), a vital precaution before setting out.

From Bardsea, the trail follows the shingle beach southeast along the shoreline to enter Bardsea Country Park (car park and picnic site) and then Sea Wood (see page 117), an ancient oak and ash woodland owned and managed by the Woodland Trust. The next point of interest is the 12th-century church at Aldingham (see page 115), believed to be the last remnant of a village now lost to coastal erosion. Be careful not to disturb the wildlife on the next section down to Moat Scar and keep an eye on the tide (the sea sometimes covers the path here at high tide).

The final stretch of the trail meanders via Newbiggin to Rampside and Roosebeck, where it leaves the foreshore (again, beware the tide: the footpath at the bottom of the cliff has no escape route at high tide) and continues around the peninsula towards Barrow-in-Furness.

Alternatively, hire bikes from the Mountain Centre (T01229-71646, mountaincentre.co.uk) in Broughton-in-Furness and follow the **Duddon Valley** (see page 146), spotting seabirds all the way to the coast.

Best of the rest

The village of **Gleaston** is worth exploring for its ruined, 14th-century stone keep and fortress. **Gleaston Watermill** (T01229-869244, watermill. co.uk, year round Tue-Sun and bank holiday Mon 1100-1600, £2.50 adult, £2 child, £6.50 family) is a restored corn mill dating from 1774. You can see the original 5.5-m-high waterwheel and the corn-

Ditch the car

There are three main trails in the South Lakes region, all of which can be broken down into short day sections for some walking or cycling.

• The Cistercian Way is a 33-mile trail through the Furness and Cartmel peninsulas, from Grange-over-Sands to Roa Island.

• The Cumbria Coastal Way is a 150-mile trail around the Cumbrian coast.

• The Walney to Wear Cycle Route is a 151-mile national trail from Barrow-in-Furness in England's Northwest to Sunderland in the Northeast.

Off the beaten track Low Furness Peninsula

Meet the King

Cut off from the mainland at the tip of Low Furness Peninsula, Piel Island is a remote and wondrous place. It has a ruined 14th-century castle, managed by English Heritage, a colony of seals, and a pub, the Ship Inn, which currently has a temporary berth while the main building undergoes long-term refurbishment. The pub's landlord is traditionally crowned the King of Piel and the current incumbent, Steve Chattaway, is to be found carefully polishing the crown jewels, with the island pretty much to himself. The main contact for information about visits to Piel Island is John Murphy (T01229-473746, murphysmiles@hotmail.com), whose company Murphy's Miles runs trips across the sands at low tide. In summer, ferry services to Piel operate from Roa Island on the mainland.

You can also camp on Piel Island – it's free – but best ask the king first.

Watch your mouth: the folk tale of Urswick Tarn

Urswick Tarn is the largest of the glacial lakes that pepper the Lower Furness Peninsula. It is home to a great variety of waterfowl, including moorhens, swans, greylag geese and the ubiquitous coot. But it harbours a dark past according to local folklore. Revolted by the slanderous gossip of the Urswick women 'from tongues that spat out black venom as night, poisoned the days, tattler and gadabouts, casting an evil eye on all', the local priest told them all to go home and keep their doors and windows open. He then induced a huge hole to appear that swallowed up their houses and filled with water to create the present-day Urswick Tarn.

mill machinery in action and learn about the self-sufficient lifestyle of the early miller. Head downstairs for a display on bee-keeping, including an observation hive where you can watch the bees at work. Also on site is the Pig's Whisper Country Store, selling local crafts, Gleaston flour and produce, and tea rooms providing wholesome meals.

Urswick Tarn, the largest glacial tarn on the peninsula, dominates the twin villages of Great and Little Urswick. The reed beds in the area are rich in wildlife, with herons, cormorants, Canadian geese and gulls amongst the regular visitors to the water's edge. If you are here at the end of September, you might catch the annual rush bearing celebrations (see page 115).

Finally, the village of **Dendron**, famed for its displays of crocuses in spring, is home to Dendron Church (1642), which doubled as a village school during its early years.

Get close to nature

Remote **Walney Island**, across the causeway from Barrow-in-Furness, has twin nature reserves, one at either end of the island, where you can spot seals, herring gulls and Natterjack toads. There are also a couple of sandy but windswept beaches to fly a kite or roam through the dunes.

Grab a bite

The **Royal Oak** in Spark Bridge, near Ulverston (LA12 8BS, T01229-861006, royaloaksparkbridge. co.uk) does decent lunches, including a mean ploughman's platter (£7.95) and hearty Sunday roasts. Another local favourite is the **White Hart Inn** at Bouth (LA12 8JB, T01229-861229, whitehart-lakedistrict.co.uk), which has cask ales and local produce on the menu (mains around £11). Try also **Millstones Farm Shop** (nr Millom, LA19 5TJ, T01229-718775, millstonesbootle.co.uk) for bakery, deli and restaurant goodies; and **Crooklands Garden Centre** (Dalton-in-Furness, LA15 8JH, T01229-464225, crooklandsgardencentre.co.uk) for home-made and seasonal produce.

Essential websites

southlakeland.gov.uk/tourism
lakedistrictoutdoors.co.uk

Ceremony to crown
the new King of Piel.

Out & about South Lakes

Action stations

Abseiling & climbing
River Deep Mountain High

Clock Tower Buildings, Low Wood, Haverthwaite, Cumbria, LA12 7QZ, T01539-528666, riverdeepmountainhigh.co.uk. Half day abseiling or climbing £40 (£30 child, 8 and under); £70 adult, £50 child (16 and under) for a multi-activity day.
Abseiling (from 10 years) and climbing (from six years) are among the activities on offer. Choose from a half day on one activity or a multi-activity full day.

Fishing
High Newton Trout Fishery

Grange-over-Sands, T01539-53285. Fly-fishing for brown and rainbow trout on an 11-acre tarn near Grange.

Horse riding
Bigland Hall Equestrian

Backbarrow, nr Newby Bridge, LA12 8PB, T01539-530333, biglandhall. com. Private child's lesson from £20/30 mins.
Set against the spectacular terrain of the Bigland Hall estate, the centre offers a full range of pony trekking and trail rides for all ages (from four years upwards) and abilities.

Crooked Birch
Equestrian Centre

Subberthwaite, nr Ulverston, T01229-885060, crookedbirch.co.uk. Rides from £30/2 hrs.
Crooked Birch is a superb base for exploring hundreds of routes and bridleways, taking riders to summits over 250 m high, with glorious panoramic views of the Lakeland fells. All abilities welcome (minimum age five years). You can even bring your own horse and simply pay for livery at £35/day.

Tennis
Promenade Recreation Ground

Grange-over-Sands.
Single tennis court available for use from April to the end of October. Contact the tourist information centre in Grange-over-Sands for details.

Experience
Morecambe Bay

Morecambe Bay is the second-largest bay in the UK and known for its huge tides. These go out very far (up to eight miles) and come in very quickly. It is a superb place for kids to hunt for shells and spot sea birds and other wildlife, such as butterflies and orchids, and part of the bay forms the Arnside/Silverdale Area of Outstanding Natural Beauty.
But while beautiful, Morecambe Bay can be a dangerous place on

How to stay safe

Care needs to be taken when walking along the coastal path of Morecambe Bay. Top tips to stay safe are:

• Take a large-scale Ordnance Survey map with you.
• Check the tide times before you set out. Tide tables can be bought from tourist information offices (also see page 5). You should be off the sand at least three hours before high tide.
• Check the weather forecast before you leave.
• Carry a mobile phone and a whistle.
• Take a compass with you.
• Wear suitable footwear and brightly coloured clothing.
• Always tell other people where you are going and what time you should be back.
• If you get stuck in quicksand, lie down, spread out your arms and legs, blow your whistle and call 999. If you see a patch of dry sand try to crawl towards it.
• Stay in contact with the local coastguard: T1051 931 3341.

account of its quicksands and fast-flowing water. It is frequently said that the tide here comes in faster than a galloping horse. Families with older children (secondary level and able to do an eight-mile walk) may enjoy the thrill of crossing the sands on a guided walk led by Cedric Robinson, MBE. The Queen's Guide to the Sands, he has been leading guided walks across the potentially hazardous sands of Morecambe Bay since 1963. The walks start from the seaside village of Arnside, about 10 miles north of Morecambe, and finish at Kents Bank. En route are fine views of the South Lakeland hills and a chance to spot communities of wading birds. Certificates are awarded to those who complete the crossing.

Book in advance via the Morecambe Visitor Information Centre (T01524-582808, citycoastcountryside.co.uk).

Essential websites

arnsidesilverdaleaonb.org.uk
citycoastcountryside.co.uk
morecambebay.org.uk

Don't miss Holker Hall & Gardens

Genteel and imposing, Holker Hall is one of Britain's quintessential stately homes and the regal abode of Lord and Lady Cavendish. Okay, we know what you're thinking: dry and dull, the kids will hate it. But look closer and you'll find it's worth giving Holker Hall a chance.

The hall itself is one for the budding young history buff, and made more compelling thanks to the absence of ropes and other barriers. Look out in the library for works by Henry Cavendish, the scientist who discovered nitric acid amongst other important scientific experiments. His antique microscope will fascinate young scientists. The Gallery offers children a chance to step back in time and see how a landed family lived.

The gardens, showcasing roses and rhododendrons, may be more appealing to parents with horticultural leanings than children, but the **Elliptical Garden**, with its unusual geometric design, and the **Meadow**, which has 24 species of native perennial wildflowers, are great open spaces for kids to let off some steam. The **Grotto**, which has a stone tunnel and limestone underpass leading to a kitchen garden, captures young imaginations. While exploring the grounds look out for the herd of fallow deer grazing in the parkland.

In fact, Holker venison is on sale at the superb **Holker Food Hall** (see page 136) along with beef and salt-marsh lamb from the estate.

But what actually sets Holker Hall apart from your common-or-garden stately pile is the emphasis on family-friendly attractions and events. There's an adventure playground for children up to

Essential information

Cark-in-Cartmel, near Grange-over-Sands, LA11 7PL, T01539-558328, holker.co.uk. Mar-Oct Sun-Fri house 1100-1600, gardens 1030-1730, £12.25 adult, £6.50 child (6-15), £34.50 family.
See also Holker Food Hall, page 136.

12 years and a cute play area for little ones. Better still, during the school holidays a host of activities are held in the courtyard and the grounds – including mask-making and seed planting. There are two sessions per day (1030-1230 and 1330-1530), priced at £2.50 per child. These are supervised workshops, so you can leave school age children to enjoy the activities while you view the house or the gardens.

Regular events during the year include Easter weekend activities, Halloween fun days in October and activities (ages three to 10) on weekends leading up to Christmas, including twilight illuminations, carol singing, storytelling, festive food and the chance to make Christmas decorations and presents.

But it is the **Holker Garden Festival**, the jewel in the crown of the summer season, which brings in the crowds in late May or early June. The horticultural showstopper also offers live entertainment, food stalls and games and activities to keep the kids busy.

The **Courtyard Café** has high chairs and is well stocked with local produce, while the gift shop sells a selection of well-made chunky wooden toys and traditional childhood games.

You can easily spend a day exploring the various attractions in the house and gardens, perhaps combining a visit here with an early supper at the nearby village of Cartmel, see pages 136 and 139.

❷ The great Holker Lime at Holker Hall is one of Cumbria's oldest trees, with a massive girth of 7.9 m. The tree was planted in the early 1600s as part of a formal planting scheme.

Holker Hall.

Out & about South Lakes

Big days out

Ducky's Park Farm

Flookburgh, nr Grange-over-Sands, LA11 7LS, T01539-559293, duckys parkfarm.co.uk. Mar-Oct from 1030, £5.50 adult, £4.50 child, £18 family. Adorable lambs, bearded baby goats, squealing piglets and snuffling pot-bellied pigs – there are plenty of cute animals to swoon over at Ducky's Park Farm, the most family-friendly option around the pensioner-oriented town of Grange. The main draw is the farm trail, which teaches kids about farming methods and animal care. The park also offers plenty of hands-on petting – and photo opportunities – of fallow deer, capybara (a kind of giant guinea pig) and raccoons. The pedal karts and bouncy castle are a good way to burn off some energy, too. Inside, there's a huge soft-play area, Daffy's Diner café and a toy shop.

Holker Hall & Gardens

See page 124.

South Lakes Wild Animal Park

Dalton-in-Furness, LA15 8JR, T01229-466086, wildanimalpark.co.uk. Year round daily 1000-1700, Nov-Feb to 1600, £11.50 adult, £8 child.
The park (follow the signs on the A590 to Barrow, heading through the centre of Dalton) is a huge area divided by three main paths named Africa, Australia and South America, with appropriate animals in each. There's also an aviary

Maya and the monkeys, South Lakes Wild Animal Park.

South Lakes Wild
Animal Park.

Visit The Dock Museum, Barrow-in-Furness

Why? This is the perfect place for grandparents to teach little 'uns about the Good Old Days, before computer games and iPods, when Barrow was the hub of the iron and steel industry. The 'Object Handling Tour' lets you get to grip with bits and pieces from the 1940s. There's also an adventure playground and walkways linked to Cumbria's Coastal Way.

Where? Barrow-in-Furness, LA14 2PW, T01229-876400, dockmuseum.org. uk. Located in central Barrow, taking the A590 or A5087, which connect to the M6 (junction 36).

How? Apr-Oct Tue-Fri 1000-1700, weekends 1100-1700, Nov-Mar Wed-Fri 1030-1600, weekends 1100-1630, free entry and free parking.

section. Try to time a visit with some of the feeding or talk times, such as hand-feeding the giraffes at 1130, tiger feeding at 1430, or the penguins' supper at 1500.

But a word of warning too; the animals roam free in some sections of the park, albeit under the supervision of staff. This can be great for budding Attenboroughs, but can be a bit scary for young children. A better bet for them may be the little train (50p per ride), which trundles past the lemurs and tigers from a safe distance.

The Maki restaurant offers a good view of the giraffes if you sit on the right-hand side by the playground. The food is pretty average mass-market fare, with adult/child meals around £6.50/£3.50. You might prefer to save a few pounds by packing a picnic and using the indoor picnic area next to the restaurant.

Furness Abbey.

More family favourites

Furness Abbey
Nr Ulverston, T01229-823420. Easter-Sep Thu-Mon 1000-1700 (daily in summer holidays), Oct-Mar Sat and Sun 1000-1600, £3.80 adult, £1.80 child.

The former home of Cistercian monks, Furness Abbey is now an English Heritage property and revels in its ruined grandeur. The ruins were celebrated by Wordsworth in his much-loved poem, *The Prelude*. Pick up the useful audio tour for the history of the site. Afterwards, unpack a picnic (tables provided) and admire the superb views.

Hit or miss?

Carnforth Station & Visitor Centre
The Railway Station, Carnforth,
LA5 9TR, T01524-735165,
carnforthstation.co.uk.
Year round 1000-1600
(closed Mon Oct-Easter).

Does a railway station qualify
as a visitor attraction? Well, yes,
Carnforth's does. This historic
railway station has been home
to steam trains since 1846 and
restored steamers, such as the
Fellsman trains (T0845-310 2458,
statesmanrail.com) still thunder
through the intersection. The
big claim to fame, however, is its
starring role in David Lean's 1945
film *Brief Encounter*, a fact celebrated
with memorabilia in the visitor centre.

Carnforth station.

Before you leave, grab a coffee in the Refreshment Room, where Celia Johnson and Trevor Howard famously
enjoyed a romantic frisson over a pot of tea, and have your picture taken underneath the famous station clock.
Overall it's great for train buffs of any age and fans of classic films; kids will love the playroom at the rear, where they
can play trains while the adults browse the gift shop.

Furness Owls
Sandscale Park, Barrow-in-Furness,
T01229-828628, furnessowls.co.uk.
Apr-Oct daily 1000-1600, £4.50 adult,
£2.50 child.

This nature park lets you get close
to the animals with a petting zoo
and owl sanctuary, plus lots of
information about conservation
projects to inspire young minds.
You could say it's a hoot. There
are over 100 kinds of owls on
display and the keepers are keen
to share their expert knowledge.
Future plans include a new reptile
house for snakes and lizards from
around the world. The café serves
drinks and simple snacks.

**Lakeland Miniature Village &
Oriental Garden**
Flookburgh, nr Grange-over-
Sands, LA11 7LE, T01539-558500,
lakelandminiaturevillage.com.
Year round from 1030, £3.50 adult,
£1.50 child.

This model village presents a
series of lovingly hand-crafted
models of Cumbrian houses
and farms, including Hill Top,
the home of Beatrix Potter. A
work-in-progress, it sums up the
landscape of the Lakes in one visit.

Vintage poster, Lakeland Motor Museum.

Rain check

Arts & crafts
• **Artcrystal**, Grange-over-Sands, LA11 6DP, T01539-535656, artcrystal.co.uk.
• **Lakes Glass Centre**, Oubas Hill, nr Ulverston, LA12 7LY, T01229-584400, cumbriacrystal.com.
• **Yew Tree Barn**, Low Newton, nr Grange-over-Sands, LA11 6JP, T01593-531498, yewtreebarn.co.uk.

Arts centres
• **Forum 28**, Barrow-in-Furness, T0871-220 6000, forumtwentyeight.co.uk.

Cinemas
• **Apollo Cinema**, Barrow-in-Furness, T0871-220 6000.
• **Roxy Cinema**, Ulverston, T01229-582340, roxyulverston.co.uk.

Indoor play & amusements
• **Fuzzy Eds**, Barrow-in-Furness, T01229-824334.
• **Play Zone**, The Custom House, Barrow-in-Furness, T01229-823823, 1abbeyroad.co.uk. (See page 138).

Indoor swimming pools
• **Lakes Leisure**, Ulverston, T01229-584110, lakesleisure.org.uk.
• **Park Leisure Centre**, Barrow-in-Furness, T01229-871146.

Museums
• **Millom Folk Museum**, Millom, LA18 5AA, T01229-772555, millomfolkmuseum.co.uk.

The 1930s Motor Garage.

Lakeland Motor Museum
Backbarrow, T015395-58509, lakelandmotormuseum.co.uk. Feb-mid-Dec 1030-1645.

The Lakeland Motor Museum has been in the grounds of Holker Hall for years, but is due to move to new, expanded premises at Backbarrow, seven miles from Holker Hall, off the A590. The new museum is scheduled to open in mid-2010 but call ahead for the latest information, including entrance fees.

The Motoring Memories collection comprises over 30,000 exhibits and traces the history of motor transport through to the present day with some fascinating memorabilia. The range of vintage models includes Alfa Romeo, Bentley, De Lorean and Vespa. Kids will love the recreation of a 1930s garage with original tools and equipment of the period. It's a delightful glimpse of the past, with petrol pumps, lubrication charts and oil dispensers.

A major part of the exhibition is the Campbell Bluebird Exhibition, which is devoted to the legacy of Sir Malcolm Campbell and his son, Donald, who captured 21 world land- and water-speed records for Great Britain. The poignant highlight is a full-size replica of the famous jet hydroplane, *Bluebird K7*, in which Donald Campbell was tragically killed while attempting to break his own water-speed record on Coniston Water on 4 January 1967 (see page 36).

Let's go to...

Ulverston

A Victorian guidebook to Britain sums up Ulverston thus: 'A neat and well-kept market town and port, delightfully situated on the Leven estuary.' In some ways not much has changed. Ulverston remains a bustling market town with a well-developed infrastructure for a family break, good walks and a calendar packed with festivals.

Ulverston is the ideal base for exploring the South Lakes, especially if you also want to combine it with the wilder West Lakes region. It is popular with walkers, hikers and bikers for its easy access to great local trails. But, most of all, it is synonymous with one man: Stan Laurel, born Arthur Stanley Jefferson in his grandparents' house in Argyle Street, Ulverston, in 1890. Stan first made his name in Hollywood silent films in the 1920s as part of the comedy duo Laurel and Hardy. A new bronze statue to the pair, unveiled in April 2009, stands by the tourist information centre on County Square. The main attraction in the town centre is the **Laurel & Hardy Museum** (see page 133), a hit with adults and children alike. Head for its tiny cinema, papered with posters and other memorabilia, to view movie clips from their silent classics; you can

❷ Stan Laurel's interests included raising ducks and hydroponic gardening (a process in which plants are grown in sand, gravel or liquid rather than soil). He once successfully cross-bred a potato and an onion, but couldn't get anyone to sample the results. More trivia from laurel-and-hardy.com.

guarantee that your children – from toddlers to teens – will be laughing.

Get your bearings
Ulverston is easily accessed from junction 36 of the M6, taking the A590 towards Barrow-in-Furness.

It is also well served by train, with the Furness Line, the scenic route from Lancaster to Carlisle, stopping at Ulverston, and connections to the West Coast Main Line at Carnforth. The station is a five-minute walk south of the town centre.

County Square is the historic heart of town, and the location of the tourist information centre (LA12 7LZ, T01229-587120, southlakeland.gov. uk/tourism, Mon-Sat 1000-1600), housed within Coronation Hall. The post office is across the square, with the best parking next to the bus station northwest of the square.

Take a walk
There's a great way to get to know Ulverston: a three-mile, two-hour stroll on easy paths from the town centre to the canal and the shores of Morecambe Bay. It's an easy-going walking trail for families with lots of history and wildlife to spot en route, such as coots, ducks and herons. You can feed the ducks on the canal and take a paddle in the stream at Bardsea if the tide is in.

The trail starts at the **Market Place**, where you can stock up on bottles of water and bars

---

Ditch the car
You can hike and bike your way around the South Lakes. Ulverston is the southern trailhead for the Cumbria Way (thecumbriaway.info), the long-distance trail that leads via Coniston and Keswick to Carlisle. The Cumbria Way Cycle Route (cumbriawaycycleroute. co.uk), developed by Sustrans, covers a similar route heading north. For bike hire, try Gill Cycles (Ulverston, LA12 7BJ, T01229-581116, gillcycles.co.uk).

COUNTRY
MARKET

HERE
NOW!

County Square, Ulverston.

Sleeping South Lakes

Cartmel Camping & Caravan Park

Wells House Farm, Cartmel, LA11 6PN, T01539-536270, ukparks.co.uk/cartmel. Mar-Oct, from £8 adult, £3 child (5-15).

Looking for a rural escape, a back-to-nature camping trip, yet one close to one of the loveliest villages in Cumbria? Step this way. Cartmel's tranquil five-acre park, with two fields for static caravans and tents, is set in achingly pretty scenery. It's also hard to beat for convenience, with a good children's playground just outside the site and a small Spar supermarket a five-minute walk away. The pubs, restaurants and attractions of Cartmel are just a short stroll along a country lane. And what a stroll it is on a fine summer evening. The site itself is well maintained, with a relaxed and friendly atmosphere.

Also recommended
Bardsea Leisure Park
Ulverston, LA12 9QE, T01229-584712, bardsealeisure.co.uk.

Birch Bank Camping Site
Blawith, nr Ulverston, LA12 8EW, T01229-885277, birchbank.co.uk.

Meathop Caravan Park
Grange-over-Sands, LA11 6RB, T01539-533596, meathopcaravans.co.uk.

South End Caravan Park
Walney Island, Barrow-in-Furness, LA14 3YQ, T01229-472823, walneyislandcaravanpark.co.uk.

Templand Farm
Allithwaite, nr Grange-over-Sands, LA11 7QX, T01539-533129, templandfarm.co.uk.

Best of the rest

Walkers Hostel
Ulverston, LA12 7LB, 01229-585588, walkershostel.co.uk. Year round, reception 1600-1800 and 2100-2230, £17.50 person.

This long-established, independent hostel, on the A590 just outside Ulverston, is a favourite spot for walkers. Bedroom five is a large family room with one double, two bunks and two singles. It's a simple, friendly place with a decent kitchen and a sunny terrace. For an additional small fee, the owners will fill flasks, make packed lunches and dry damp clothes.

Witherslack Hall Farmhouse
Witherslack, nr Grange-over-Sands, LA11 6SD, T01539-552244, witherslackhallfarmhouse.co.uk. This former 17th-century manor house turned rural guesthouse also has an adjoining riding centre, with pony trekking suitable for over-sevens.

Rent a cottage

The South Lakes lends itself well to self-catering breaks, with a good range of cottages and an abundance of great local food readily available. These are some of the best self-catering cottages:

Grange End Cottage
Cark-in-Cartmel, nr Grange-over-Sands, LA11 7NZ, T01524-702955, holidaycottagescumbria.com.

Hardcragg Hall
Grange-over-Sands, LA11 6BJ, T01539-533353, hardcragghall.co.uk.

The Hayloft
Allithwaite, nr Grange-over-Sands, LA11 7RH, T01524-221390, hayloftcottageholidays.co.uk.

Hazelwood Court self-catering
Grange-over-Sands, LA11 6SP, T01539-534196, hazelwoodcourt.co.uk.

Stockdale Farm
Flookburgh, nr Grange-over-Sands, LA11 7LR, T01229-889601, southlakes-cottages.com.

Wolf House Cottages
Silverdale, nr Carnforth, LA5 0TX, T01524-701573, wolfhousecottages.co.uk.

The Bay Horse Hotel

Ulverston, LA12 9EL, T01229-583972, thebayhorsehotel.co.uk.

Old Daltongate House

Ulverston, LA12 7BD, T01229-588328, ulverstonbandb.co.uk

St Mary's Mount Manor House

Ulverston, T01229-849005, stmarysmount.co.uk.

Splashing out

Hampsfell House Hotel

Grange-over-Sands, LA11 6BG, T01539-532567, hampsfellhouse. co.uk. From £75/room B&B, plus £7.50 child 0-6 sharing, £12.50 child 6-12 sharing.

Like much of Grange, this hotel is rather twee and old fashioned, but it's a practical base set in private grounds. The nine rooms, including a designated family room, may look a little faded but the bathrooms are smarter, albeit in some cases with a bath but no shower. For a pleasant stroll after dinner, Eggerslack Wood (see page 117) is just on the doorstep.

Lonsdale House Hotel

Ulverston, LA12 7BD, T01229-582598, lonsdalehousehotel.co.uk. From £85/room B&B.

The only hotel in Ulverston town centre, the Lonsdale House is a traditional property with two family suites and a good range of well-equipped doubles. Room

Lonsdale House Hotel.

231 is particularly well suited to families, with a fold-out sofa bed and a large jacuzzi bath. Count on a good breakfast in the morning, served in the Eleven Restaurant in the cellar.

Lymehurst Hotel

Grange-over-Sands, LA11 7EY, T01539-533076, lymehurst.co.uk. From £100/room B&B, plus £20 child sharing.

Attempting to move with the times more than other Grange properties, the Lymehurst is a smarter option with contemporary rooms and good in-house dining in the Lymestone restaurant. Expect a good breakfast with an emphasis on local produce and some interesting fusion options on the dinner menu. Superior

and deluxe doubles can be converted to family rooms with a Z bed.

Also recommended

Bankfield House

Millom, LA18 5LL, T01229-772276, bankfieldhouse.com.

Duke of Edinburgh Hotel

Barrow-in-Furness, LA14 5QR, T01229-821039, dukeofedinburghhotel.co.uk.

No 43

Arnside, LA5 0AA, T01524-762761, no43.org.uk.

135

Eating South Lakes

Local goodies

Cartmel Village Shop

Cartmel, T01539-536201, cartmelvillageshop.co.uk. Mon-Sat 0900-1700, Sun 1000-1630.
Cartmel draws devotees from far and wide to worship at the shrine of sticky toffee pudding – sales of over 100,000 puddings per month speak volumes. The Village Shop has been making the pudding to its secret recipe for generations and, while the bakery has now moved elsewhere, it still guards the recipe closely. Aside from the freezer cabinet full of sticky puddings (chocolate, ginger banana and Christmas puddings too), the shop has the usual range of upscale delicatessen fare with local ales, preserves and delicious smoked meats.

Higginsons

Grange-over-Sands, LA11 6AB, T01539-534367.
Quite simply the best butcher around for locally sourced meats.

Holker Food Hall

Cark-in-Cartmel, near Grange-over-Sands, LA11 7PL, T01539-558328, holkerfoodhall.co.uk. Feb-Dec 1030-1730 (1600 in low season).
Renowned for its flavoursome lamb, reared on the saltmarshes of Holker Hall's estate, this sumptuous food hall is also the place to go for tasty local cheeses and other gourmet fare. There's a great selection of local ales, some specially brewed for the food hall, plus the region's ubiquitous sticky toffee pudding.

Market days

Ulverston, Market Place, every Thursday and third Saturday.

Holme Farm Ice Cream

Grange-over-Sands, LA11 6QX, T01539-535991.
The farm has over 10 flavours of ice cream, including the award-winning honeycomb and liquorice flavour, all produced using milk from the farm's pedigree Holstein cows.

Howbarrow Organic Farm

Cartmel, LA11 7SS, T01539-536330, howbarroworganic.co.uk. Wed-Sat 1000-1700.
A superb farm shop, selling organic fruit and vegetable boxes. Also check out the Farm Trail to stretch your legs before stocking up.

Cartmel Village Shop, the place to go for sticky toffee pudding.

Templand Farm Shop

Allithwaite, nr Grange-over-Sands, LA11 7QX, T01539-533129, templandfarm.co.uk.
Selling a range of home-produced meats and vegetables and other locally sourced foods.

Woodall's of Waberthwaite

Waberthwaite, nr Millom, LA19 5YJ, T01229-717237, richardwoodall.com.
Breakfast bangers by royal appointment, plus cured hams and bacon.

Also recommended
Airey's Farm Shop

Ayside, nr Grange-over-Sands, LA11 6JE, T01539-531237, aireysfarmshop. co.uk. Closed Sun.
Local meats, including dry-cured bacons and award-winning Cumberland sausage, are the ones to buy.

Quick & simple

Butterfingers

Grange-over-Sands, T01539-532745. Mon-Sat 0900-1700, Sun 1000-1600.
A cheap but cheerful little café for breakfast rolls, snack lunches (around £7) and kids' meals (around £4). Situated on the road to the train station from the town centre. It's low-frills stuff but does what it says on the tin.

Cavendish Arms

Cartmel, LA11 6QA, T01539-936240, thecavendisharms.co.uk.
The pick of the pubs in Cartmel, this charming, 450-year-old

coaching inn serves up some great British fare with a hint of gastropub finesse. It's a cosy spot with antique furnishings, wood beams and a roaring log fire in winter. In summer, there's a lovely beer garden featuring hanging baskets, ablaze with colour, and chunky wooden tables for a sundowner. Tuck into hearty, locally sourced main meals (around £14).

Gillam's

Ulverston, LA12 7LT, T01229-587564. Mon-Sat 0900-1700, Sun 0900-1600.
Owned by the Gillam family since 1892, this delightful tearoom in the heart of town serves up tasty, traditional food using organic ingredients. It's a proudly microwave-free zone. The delicious vegetarian, vegan and gluten-free options are best enjoyed in the quiet garden away from the staccato clinking of china teacups inside. They do a marvellous Little Gillam's Tea Party for under-12s (£3.75) and serve a Tea Guild-approved afternoon tea for £6.95, both including sandwiches, scones and cakes. A caffeine boost of Sumatran-blend coffee costs £1.95. Sit back, tuck in and enjoy.

Hazelmere Café & Bakery

Grange-over-Sands, T015395-32972, hazelmerecafe.co.uk. Daily 1000-1700.
A supremely old-school café and bakery, located opposite the ornamental gardens and near the promenade, the Hazelmere

Sample
specialities

The Cartmel region is renowned for its Cumbrian specialities. Make sure you put these three on your shopping list:

• **Flookburgh potted shrimps**
Morecambe Bay is famous for its delectable potted shrimps and Flookburgh is one of the main centres for catching and processing the catch.

• **Saltmarsh lamb**
Bred on the low-lying salt marshes around the Cartmel Peninsula, the lamb has a distinctive sweet, delicate flavour that is highly prized.

• **Cumberland Sausage**
Award-winning traditional Cumberland sausages can be found at a number of butchers and farm shops in the area.

is the domain of china cups, silver strainers and starched uniforms. It was the 2009 winner of the British Tea Guild's Award of Excellence and prides itself on home-baked cakes using organic flour, fresh cream and full-fat butter. Try a Cumberland Rum Nicky, a traditional Lakeland recipe of dates, cherries and rum, and work your way through the huge range of teas from around the world, ranging from a Gisoru Estate, Rwanda, to a Hojicha Kyushu from Japan. Look out, too, for the box of kids' books by the door to keep little 'uns busy while you pour your cuppa.

Eating South Lakes

Rose & Crown
Cartmel, LA111 7NU, T01539-558051.
Located on the market square in the heart of the village, this is a no-nonsense spot popular with families. Serves local ales and simple pub grub, with daily mains around £10, decent kids' meals (£5.95) and a Sunday roast with all the trimmings for £7.95 from 1200 onwards.

Also recommended
The Custom House
Barrow-in-Furness, LA14 5UF, T01229-823823.
A modern restaurant, bar and internet café with family leisure activities, including PlayZone, an indoor play area suitable for children aged one to eight, and LazerZone for over-eights.

Posh nosh

L'Enclume
Cartmel, LA 11 6PZ, T01539-536362, lenclume.co.uk. Lunch Wed–Sun 1200-1330, dinner daily 1830–2100.
Cartmel may seem an unlikely spot for a Michelin-starred

restaurant with rooms, but Simon Rogan's Lakeland empire offers just that. L'Enclume can give Heston Blumenthal's Fat Duck a run for its money, with its surreal menu of unfathomably titled dishes, and prices are not too high. Too esoteric for you? See Rogan & Company, L'Enclume's relaxed and informal sister, below.

Rogan & Company
LA11 6QD, T01539-535917, roganandcompany.co.uk, daily from 0900.
Simon Rogan's more accessible spin-off venture (also see L'Enclume, above) combines high-quality local produce, budget-conscious prices and, crucially, a child-friendly approach for families with a penchant for fine food.

Fish & chips

There's only one place for a fish supper in the South Lakes: the seaside **Arnside Chip Shop** (Arnside, T01524-761874, arnsidechipshop.co.uk, Tue-Sat 1130-1400 and 1630-2030, Sun 1200-1930). It boasts the venerable title of South Lakeland Chip Shop of the Year 2009 and offers unrivalled views of Morecambe Bay while you tuck into a haddock

and chips or one of the pies or puddings. The specials are served with tea, bread, chips and mushy peas – all for a bargain £7. With a big range of kids' meals (£3.25), plus gluten-free batter and vegetarian options, this is one old-school classic not afraid to move with the times. Just be sure to save some room for an ice-cream sundae (£7).

❷ Cartmel sticky toffee pudding is the favourite dessert of both celebrity chef Jean Christophe Novelli and Madonna.

The menu is diverse and proudly regional with mains of local steak, lamb and fish for around £14. Also worth a try are the Lakeland Platters – choose a selection of local smoked fish or cured meats for £10.95. Ask the friendly staff about child portions, but be aware that dinner service does not start until 1830. Situated just south of Cartmel's main square by the river.

Opposite page: The Custom House play area.

Contents

West Lakes

Buttermere.

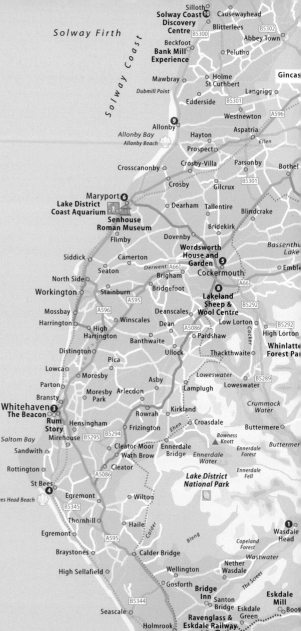

The attractions of western Cumbria may be less publicized and more scattered than those in the rest of the Lake District but they are no less compelling. Think majestic mountains, luminous lakes, rushing rivers and, crucially for the

Yewbarrow, Wasdale.

west, a strip of crisp coastline with rock pools to investigate and long sandy beaches for building sandcastles and flying kites.

The West is not without its share of top attractions, some of them slyly stealing the thunder of the better known Central Lakes. Britain's favourite view? That'll be **Wasdale Head**. Britain's most secluded lake? That'll be **Ennerdale**, then. Two of northern Britain's finest beaches? Step forward **St Bees** and **Allonby**. And Britain's biggest liar? He, or she, is crowned annually at the Bridge Inn in far western Cumbria. And that's no lie.

Historically western Cumbria was closely linked to the Roman Empire, the northern frontier of which was defined by the building of Hadrian's Wall between Tynemouth (Wallsend) and the Solway Firth. All that remains today is **Ravenglass Roman Bath House** and **Hardknott Roman Fort**, especially worth visiting if the kids are learning about the Romans at school.

Civilizations have come and gone, and nowadays it's tribes of tourists that are slowly encroaching on the territory. The obvious base for visitors is **Cockermouth**, a town full of character and the location of **Wordsworth House and Garden**, a delightfully unconventional National Trust site where children can join in the fun of recreating an 18th-century family home. Alternatively, **Whitehaven** is enjoying a renaissance, with a maritime museum and a new harbourside development filled with artworks and cool new cafés. Finally, **Ravenglass** is within easy reach of **Muncaster Castle** and **La'al Ratty**, the two must-do family excursions.

Get away from the towns, and you'll soon experience the raw force and beauty of nature. The **Solway Coast** Area of Outstanding Natural Beauty (AONB) is a haven for wading birds and other wildlife, and has a gloriously remote, end-of-the-earth quality. Several nature reserves here have easy walks, some accessible with a pushchair or wheelchair, that are good for spotting dragonflies, butterflies, wild flowers and a wide variety of birds

Other regions of the Lakes offer familiar charms, but way out west feels like another world. More information about the region from western-lakedistrict.co.uk.

Out & about West Lakes

Set your eyes on England's best view

A TV programme in 2007 proclaimed the view from Wastwater to be the best view in England. Rightly so. For the best scenery in the West Lakes – all of it free to enjoy – the Wasdale Valley is the one to head for. When a blazing-red sunset glimmers along the water's edge, it's nothing short of magical.

To capture the sunset at Wasdale Head, turn left on the A595 at Gosforth and head inland. While there, the kids may like to visit St Olaf's, Britain's smallest church, a little gem with Viking origins.

Aside from award-winning views and a record-beating church, the Wasdale Valley has England's deepest lake at 79 m (Wastwater) and its highest mountain at 978 m (Scafell Pike). The valley is crisscrossed by walking trails. Teenagers may enjoy the challenge of well-trodden trails such as Great Gable, Scoat Fell and Lingmell, plus the triumph of scaling Scafell Pike. None of these is suitable for young children.

More from visitcumbria.com/wc/wastwtr.htm.

In November 2009 the West Lakes was hit by one of the worst storms in living memory. Cockermouth was the place worst affected, but Workington, Keswick and smaller villagers were also badly hit.

Visit Cumbria's most secluded lake

The next valley across from Wasdale, Ennerdale is often described as the most scenic enclave of the Lake District National Park. The 2½-mile-long lake is the furthest west and not encircled by road – so you can't drive around it. However, you can park up at Bowness Knot, the trailhead for several good walks, including the Smithy Beck Trail, the one best suited to families. The gentle two-mile route follows the lakeshore and heads deep into the Ennerdale Forest, perfect for collecting leaves, conkers and acorns in autumn.

❸ A large population of garden gnomes lives at the bottom of Wastwater – placed there by divers over the years.

View from Wastwater

Discover
Great Lakes

Sour Milk Gill.

The West Lakes are brooding and remote, with spectacular scenery but limited access and few leisure facilities or strategically placed ice cream vans. They're a good place to get away from the crowds, take a picnic and find that perfect skimmer. But check the weather forecast first.

Wastwater
At nearly three miles long, almost half a mile wide and, with a depth of 79 m, Wastwater is England's deepest lake. It is flanked by scree slopes and dominated by a clutch of towering peaks, including England's highest mountain, Scafell Pike.

Buttermere
A short stroll from the car park leads you to the northern end of the lake where the shore is littered with skimming stones. Nearby, the mere overflows into a small river (perfect for stick-racing), while Sour Milk Gill, tumbling from Red Pike, is another diversion. Sooner or later, though, the four-mile circuit around Buttermere beckons. It's an easy walk, with peaks looming all around.

Crummock Water
Like Buttermere, Crummock boasts superb views. It is a clear, rocky-bottomed lake flanked by steep fell sides of Skiddaw slate.

Loweswater
In the Vale of Lorton in the far west, Loweswater is one of the most peaceful lakes.

Ennerdale Water
This is the most westerly of the lakes. As well as the Smithy Beck Trail (see left), a low-level eight-mile circuit of the lake is suitable for older children who are good walkers.

Out & about West Lakes

Take a boat trip from Whitehaven harbour.

The Forestry Commission is working to return parts of the valley to its original state by bringing in wild cattle and limiting the timber trade as part of the Wild Ennerdale Project (wildennerdale.co.uk).

Make a splash in a Roman bath

The Roman bathhouse, also known as Walls Castle, near the harbour in Ravenglass makes for a free afternoon out for children interested in the Romans. The former fort of Glannaventa was an essential link to the garrisons stationed along Hadrian's Wall, and its bathhouse, a must-have for any self-respecting Roman legionaries, is one of the best-preserved bathhouses in Britain. If you're heading on to Hadrian's Wall country (see page 94), this will give you a taste of what's to come.

Take a hike in the Duddon Valley

This is a delightful hidden gem deep in the heart of farming country, where livestock outnumber the local residents

by a considerable factor. It's also good walking country. Work up an appetite for a picnic with a short hike up to Wallowbarrow Crag from Seathwaite. For an easier walk with small children, explore Dunnerdale Forest or enjoy a riverbank walk along the River Duddon. More from duddonvalley.co.uk.

Get back to nature

For birdwatching, family walks, picnics and getting back to nature, the Watch Tree Nature Reserve (Great Orton, T 01228-712539, watchtree. co.uk) is seven miles west of Carlisle, between the villages of Kirkbampton and Wiggonby, between the B5307 and A596 respectively. Catch one of the guided walks on Thursdays from April to September, at 1900.

Explore the maritime history of Whitehaven

The port of Whitehaven (whitehaven.org.uk) was once the third largest port in the UK. It has long since fallen from favour as a hub for trade, but a brand new marina and harbourside

development has put a new spring in its step. There are smart places to eat and drink and a new maritime museum (see page 156). Tall ships pay a visit to the town for the maritime festival in June – a great family day out – and there are always boat trips and fishing excursions.

Best beaches

A day at the seaside might not be something that naturally springs to mind when visiting the Lake District. It's hard to see beyond all those mountains and lakes. But Cumbria is home to over 90 miles of coastline and has some wonderfully unspoilt beaches, especially in western Cumbria. Several of the more remote beaches offer great places to roll out the picnic blanket, fly a kite, chase a frisbee or while away a magical afternoon net-dipping in the rock pools.

Allonby

Head north beyond Maryport and you'll find Allonby, which has far-reaching views over to Scotland and the Isle of Man. The village has a wide crescent-shaped bay with a sand and shingle beach, which at low tide becomes a vast expanse of sand that's ideal for kite-flying, beach games and paddling.

Allonby evolved from a fishing village to become a

fashionable sea-bathing resort, and in 1835 its fine Georgian façades were joined by the grand Victorian Baths, a suite of heated saltwater pools for bathing, now converted to private homes. Today the beach is best known for Twentyman's ice cream shop with its irresistible home-made ice cream (see page 168) in a multitude of flavours.

🕙 Throughout the Middle Ages, smuggling was rife along the Solway coast. Allonby was at the heart of the action with goods such as spirits, tobacco and fine textiles regularly smuggled in from Scotland, Ireland and the Isle of Man.

St Bees

If you're lucky at St Bees, you might spot porpoises, basking sharks or seals. Four miles south of Whitehaven, St Bees is the starting point of the long-distance Coast to Coast walking route to Robin Hood's Bay in North Yorkshire. It has a long sandy beach with rock pooling and shell hunting near the base of St Bees Head. The beach slopes gently and offers good swimming away from the headlands.

You can get good views of the seabirds that nest on the red sandstone bluff either by joining a boat trip from Whitehaven (see page 152), or following the cliff-top path towards Fleswick Bay. The St Bees Head Nature Reserve (rspb.org.uk) has the largest seabird colony on the west coast of England, home to over 5000 breeding birds, including puffins, kittiwakes, guillemots and razorbills.

Allonby beach.

Let's go to...

Cockermouth

The handsome Georgian town of Cockermouth is attractively located between the rivers Derwent and Cocker on the edge of the Lake District National Park. It makes a good family base with lots of infrastructure, several worthwhile attractions within easy reach and plenty of good places to eat, drink and sleep.

Cockermouth was one of the earliest towns in the area to be granted a market charter in 1226 and retains its regional market town status today. The broad, tree-lined main thoroughfare, Main Street, is home to a good mix of traditional coaching inns, cosy cafés and practical, independent shops.

❷ Cockermouth enjoyed a Georgian building boom between 1720 and 1830, a period of prosperity when many of its most famous sons were born. William Wordsworth is the best known local, but his contemporaries include Fletcher Christian (1764–1793), leader of the mutiny on *The Bounty*; John Dalton (1766–1844), inventor of atomic theory; and Fearon Fallows (1789–1831), the Astronomer Royal.

Historically, Cockermouth had a thriving industrial base, with several mills producing woollen, linen and cotton goods, notably the Derwent Mill with its Harris embroidery. In 1874, the Jennings Brewery (established in 1828 by Jenning Brothers in Lorton) relocated to

Cockermouth. It continues to brew their traditional real ales in the same location today and now acts as a tourist attraction for the town.

Most recently, however, Cockermouth made the headlines as a victim of severe weather conditions. The rivers Derwent and Cocker broke their banks in November 2009, leading to the worst flooding in the western Lakes in living memory. Cockermouth bore the brunt of the natural disaster and efforts to return some sense of normal working life to the area are likely to continue for some time.

Get your bearings

Cockermouth lies just outside the boundary of the national park and serves as the northwestern gateway from the Central Lakes, with good transport connections. It lies some 30 miles from junction 40 of the M6 (take the A66 via Keswick and Bassenthwaite Lake) and 30 miles southwest of Carlisle. The A66 runs on to Workington, the A595 branches southwest to Whitehaven, and the A596 leads northeast to Maryport and the sandy coastline stretching north to Allonby and Silloth. For parking in Cockermouth, try the pay-and-

display locations next to the Town Hall or the large car park next to the Sainsbury's supermarket at the top of Station Road.

The nearest train stations are at Carlisle and Penrith with connections to the West Coast Main Line; bus services run to and from Cockermouth to connect with national rail services.

The starting place to gather information about the town and the wider region is Cockermouth's **Tourist Information Centre** (Market Street, CA13 9NP, T01900-822634, cockermouthtic@co-net.com; Jan-Mar and Nov-Dec Mon-Fri 0930-1600, Sat 1000-1400, Apr-Jun and Sep-Oct Mon-Sat 0930-1630, Jul-Aug Mon-Sat 0930-1700, Sun 1000-1400). It is housed in a splendid 19th-century building, once a Weslyan Chapel, adjoining the Town Hall on the eastern fringe of town.

Walk the Cockermouth Town Trail

To soak up the heritage of Cockermouth and introduce kids to local history, the **Town Trail** leads to some interesting nooks and crannies with wall plaques at key points. It can be made more fun by turning it into a treasure hunt. The

Let's go to... Cockermouth

leaflet *Cockermouth Town Trail*, produced by the Cockermouth and District Civic Trust, is available from the tourist information centre (see above), and includes the following highlights:

Cockermouth Castle

The town's Norman castle is privately owned by the Dowager Lady Egremont, and is not normally open to the public. During Cockermouth's summer festival, however, Lady Egremont flings open the doors for tours (pre-booking is essential) to let children have a glimpse of life in an historic castle. Contact the tourist information centre for more details.

Memorial Gardens

A haven of open space with a children's playground next to the River Derwent. It overlooks the rear of Wordsworth House.

Harris Park

A large open space in which to run around, with superb views across the town. Also has tennis courts and a bowling green.

Kirkgate Centre

The building began life in 1868 as a school but was converted into the town's main arts and entertainment centre in the 1990s. Today it stages films, shows and events, including some children's activities and shows during school holidays.

Lakeland Livestock Centre

The Market Place has been the hub of Cockermouth life for centuries and still plays host to a working livestock market every Wednesday and every other Friday. Visitors are welcome to attend free of charge, offering kids a good chance to learn about local food production, animal breeds and life on the local farms.

All Saint's Church

For families following the Wordsworth Trail (see page 50), this imposing Victorian church, built in

(see page 50)

Don't miss

After exploring the town, pop into **Neo's Gallery and Coffee Shop** (Market Place, T01900-829900, neosgallery.com), a popular arts centre with a thriving gallery for local artists and a café with regular poetry and music events.

1854, has a towering spire and a large stained-glass window in tribute to William Wordsworth. His father, John Wordsworth, is buried in the churchyard.

Stock up at a local shop

Cockermouth is known for its small independent shops, a far cry from the mass-market high-street chains that pepper so many British towns and cities. Some of the best include: **Knitting Fever** (Main St, T01900-822222) which sells beautiful hand-knitted Aran sweaters, babywear, shawls and pram covers; **Firns Home Hardware** (Station St, T01900-823123, firns.co.uk), a traditional hardware and ironmongers; **Bitter Beck Pottery** (Market Place, T07803-174120, bitterbeck.co.uk), a showcase for the decorative stoneware of the artist Joan Hardie; **Percy House Gallery** (Market Place, T01900-829667, percyhouse.co.uk), located in Percy House, Cockermouth's oldest surviving town house, which showcases work by local artists, from pewterware to photography; and **JB Banks & Son ironmongers** (Market Place, T01900-822281, jbbanks.co.uk), founded in 1836, a Victorian gem, with rows of wooden drawers behind the mahogany counter, an ornate vintage till and old lamps hanging from the ceiling. But it's still also a working shop with key cutting, ironmongery and hardware.

Essential websites

cockermouth.org.uk
western-lakedistrict.co.uk

For kids, Wordsworth is probably some old bloke who wrote boring poetry. So how is the house a family attraction?
We pride ourselves on being a family-friendly destination. I can see older children being hauled in, dragging their feet, but they've completely changed their view by the end of the visit. The Wordsworth House may be a National Trust property but it's not some dusty, dry museum closed off behind ropes and 'do not touch' signs. It's very hands on. Personally, I'd never had so much fun being paid to dress up as Amy the maidservant, chat to visitors and help to bring the house to life. I find it's the everyday things that really fascinate people.

It's clearly an educational visit but it's not a classroom-style experience?
We do start with the National Curriculum and try to work with creative writing, green issues, art and craft, science and music. But it's education by stealth. We have designed trails around the house for children, such as the wooden animal safari; we have lots of dressing-up activities with replica costumes; and children can help the servants in the kitchen or pick a posy with the gardener. During school holidays, we arrange additional activities, such as a talk on the horrors of Edwardian dentistry, or traditional Cumbrian ghost tales.

What kind of place is Cockermouth?
It's a really bustling little place and it hasn't succumbed to high-street uniformity. I love the traditional market-town feel and the great local shops such as JB Banks & Son and the Percy House Gallery.
It's also a place with a great sense of history, from the Brewery Bridge, first opened in 1897, to the Old Hall, the site of Cockermouth Hall, a pre-Elizabethan building where Mary, Queen of Scots once stayed.

Alex Morgan, Acting Custodian for the Wordsworth House and Garden, Cockermouth, CA13 9RX, T01900-820884, wordsworthhouse.org.uk.

Out & about West Lakes

Boat trips
Riptide
Whitehaven, T01946-822679/07969 327835, whitehaven.org.uk/riptide.html. £65 for up to 6 people (more for larger parties), adult £15.
Two-hour boat trip around St Bees Head. Takes in the RSPB bird sanctuary and porpoise-spotting.

Ventures West
Maryport, T01900-819439, ventureswest.co.uk. Apr-Oct £20 adult, £15 child.
Exhilarating 45-minute powerboat rides in the Solway. Based at Maryport Marina.

Cycling
Cyclewise Whinlatter
Braithwaite, CA12 5TW, T01768-778711, cyclewise.co.uk. £15/3-hr bike hire, £90/3-hr guided rides with an instructor.
The company, based in the Whinlatter Forest Park (see page opposite), offers a family skills programme to build confidence and master new cycling skills. Suitable for children aged eight and above.

Fishing
Brayton Carp Pond
Brayton, nr Aspatria, CA7 3SX, T01697-323539.
After fishing in one of the few remaining wild carp ponds in Great Britain, leave a contribution in the honesty box near the Lakeside Inn. Children under 12 do not need a rod licence. Older children (12-17) need a junior licence, which can be obtained from post offices, as can adult licences.

Horse riding
Cumbrian Heavy Horses
Chappels Farm, nr Millom, LA18 5LY, T01229-777764, cumbrianheavyhorses.com. From £50/90-min farm ride, £145/full-day fell ride.
Home to Clydesdales, Shires and Ardennes horses, this farm in the scenic Whicham Valley offers riding for all abilities. Options include farm rides, excursions to local beaches, which are ideal for cantering, and long treks across the fells; riding holiday packages are also available.

Murthwaite Green Trekking
Silecroft, Millom, T01229-770876, murthwaitegreen.co.uk. £31 mixed ability 2-hr beach ride, £42-60 beach picnic ride.
Beach rides for all abilities (aged four and above) are a speciality of this family-run riding stables. It has access to the five-mile stretch of sand and shallow waters at Silecroft beach.

Watch Hill Equestrian
Watch Hill, nr Aspatria, CA7 3SB, T07730-476836. From £20/45-min ride, £35/pony day.
Offers escorted pony trekking, lessons and hacks for all abilities from beginners to more experienced riders, aged four and above. Special pony days are available during school holidays.

Karting
West Coast Karting
Maryport, CA15 8NF, T01900-816472, westcoastkarting.co.uk. From £16 adult, £14 child.
An indoor karting facility with races, prizes and scaled-down go-karts suitable for children aged eight and above. Kids' karts have 25 mph maximum speed.

Multi activities
Adventures
Cockermouth, CA13 0JE, T01900-829775, adventures.org.uk. Call for latest offers.
Range of challenging activities for all ages and abilities. Include sailing, canoeing, rafting, abseiling, rock climbing and orienteering.

Water sports
Euphoria Extreme
Ireby, nr Wigton, CA7 1DX, T01697-371087, euphoriaextreme.com. From £50/2-hr taster session.
Kite surfing with lessons for beginners and advanced levels with no upper or lower age limits; all equipment provided.

Bike & hike the West Lakes

The west is a superb region to explore by bike or on foot. Some of the best trails are listed below.

Bike it

C2C (Sea to Sea) cycle route
Sustrans routes 7 and 71.
A 136-mile route of minor roads, cycle paths and off-road tracks from Workington to the finish at Sunderland (or Newcastle). It is particularly good for families.
c2c-guide.co.uk

Hadrian's Cycleway
Sustrans route 72.
A 174-mile long route between Ravenglass and Tynemouth that passes through the Solway Coast AONB. The Hadrian's Wall bus (service AD 122) can carry up to two bicycles per bus. Not all of the route is off-road, so care should be taken.
cycle-routes.org/hadrianscycleway

Reivers Cycle Route
Sustrans route 10.
A 172-mile trail of history and scenery in Border Reiver country between the North coast and the Irish Sea. It begins in Tynemouth and ends in Whitehaven, passing through the centre of Workington en route. It is hard-going in places, so better suited to older children and

more experienced cyclists.
reivers-guide.co.uk

West Cumbria Cycle Network
The network comprises 72 miles of cycle routes linking off-road sections with disused railway lines and minor back roads. One branch links Workington with Maryport. This is another good route for families, with lots of scenic spots en route to rest and unpack the picnic.

Hike it

Cumbria Coastal Way
This trail follows 150 miles of footpaths close to the Cumbrian shoreline from Silverdale on the border with Lancashire to the Scottish border near Gretna (or Carlisle). The route passes through Silloth, Newton Arlosh, Kirkbride and Burgh-by-Sands. The best section for families is the seven-mile stretch from Whitehaven to St Bees.
cumbriacoastalway.co.uk.

Hadrian's Wall Path National Trail
This trail follows the historic course of the Wall between Bowness-on-Solway and Wallsend at Tynemouth (via Port Carlisle, Glasson, Drumburgh and Burgh-by-Sands). It is suitable for all ages and has plenty of infrastructure along the way, including places to stay.
hadrians-wall.org.uk.

Silloth Sea, Sand and Shingle Stroll
This trail is based around three easy routes that look at different ecological habitats around Silloth. Pick up a leaflet from the tourist information centre in Silloth.

More on walking routes from lakedistrictoutdoors.co.uk.

Bikes to go

• 4Play Cycles, Cockermouth, CA13 9NH, T 01900-823377, 4playcycles.net.
• Haven Cycles, Whitehaven, CA28 9DL, T 01946-63263, havencycles@yahoo.co.uk.
More on cycling in Cumbria from cyclingcumbria.co.uk

Whinlatter Forest Park
The forest park near Cockermouth boasts some 32 miles of forest roads and tracks, hence great opportunities for walking and cycling, as well as horse riding and orienteering. The Altura cross-country route has become one of the UK's hottest mountain-biking trails. It's also the longest track in the Lakes, a 12-mile 'red' route with nine miles of single track for experienced mountain bikers. More family friendly is the 4½-mile 'blue' route designed for beginners. There is also a café, toilets and ample parking, and a walking map can be obtained from the visitor centre (T 01768-778469, forestry.gov.uk/whinlatterforestpark), which also has a video link to the osprey nest at Bassenthwaite Lake (see page 32).

Don't miss Ravenglass & Eskdale Railway

The perfect way to experience the Lake District's coast and mountains in a single day, this narrow-gauge railway chuffs seven miles between Ravenglass and Dalegarth-for-Boot. It puffs history with every toot of its whistle, and children and adults love it.

The railway (known locally as 'La'al Ratty') opened in 1875 to carry iron ore from the mine at Boot to Ravenglass. It was the first narrow-gauge railway to be built in England.

The railway fell into decline when the quarries closed but was saved in 1960 by a group of railway enthusiasts. Today the trains terminate at Dalegarth, passing the picturesque station at Irton Road, roe deer grazing near Eskdale Green and buzzards swooping over Harter Fell near Beckfoot.

It's a 40-minute journey each way, with the open-top carriages providing head-spinning views of Miterdale and Eskdale.

Travel with Postman Pat or Peter Rabbit

As well as the regular train journeys, La'al Ratty runs a packed programme of day excursions throughout the year.

These include a Children's Fun Weekend with Peter Rabbit in May, a Postman Pat day out in September and a festive Santa Express ride in the run-up to Christmas. There are also children's party deals at Dalegarth station and special train-and-bike excursions for parents and children aged 10 and above, combining a steam train ride with a three-hour cycle ride through unspoilt valleys.

> ❷ La'al Ratty is Cumbrian dialect for 'little track', referring to the narrow-gauge (15 inch/38 cm) track of the Ravenglass & Eskdale Railway.

To complete the heritage rail experience, Ravenglass station is home to the **Ravenglass Railway Museum**, which charts the railway's history and its pivotal role in the area's industrial growth. Over at **Dalegarth** station, a new play area, with a climbing frame in the shape of a train station, was opened in September 2009, providing additional entertainment to the Romans in Eskdale exhibition and the Fellbites café (see page 170).

You can travel to Ravenglass by train on the Cumbrian Coast Line and save money in the process by buying a through ticket for La'al Ratty. More details from Northern Rail (T0845-748 4950, northernrail.org).

Ravenglass railway sign.

ENGLAND'S FIRST NARROW GAUGE RAILWAY

"The Gauge for Railways of the Future"

From 1870 new railways over the world from West Africa to Japan and New Zealand had narrow tracks

Railway Gauges Compared

Standard	Narrow	Minimum
1435mm	900mm	381mm
4ft 8 1/2 ins	3ft	1ft 3ins

Most early railways followed George Stephenson's ideas in using a track about 1435 mm between the rails. That became the world Standard Gauge.

It was expensive to build, especially in mountain areas. A narrow gauge track could be laid cheaply round sharp curves, but still handle useful loads.

The Contractor Ambrose Oliver took half the shares in the new railway and hired 50 navvies under Ganger George Cleaver and Engineer Robert Nunn. Work started up Irton Road by Christmas they reached Irton Road.

Eskdale railway in spring.

Essential information

Ravenglass, T01229-717171, ravenglass-railway.co.uk.
Mar-Nov, plus winter weekends. Unlimited day travel
£10.80 adult, £5.40 child (5-15), £27.50 family.

The Beacon

Whitehaven, CA28 7LY, T01946-592302, thebeacon-whitehaven.co.uk. Year round Tue-Sun and bank holiday Mon 1000-1630, £5 adult, £4 child (under-16s free with paying adult).

This distinctive harbourside building has five floors of interactive galleries exploring Whitehaven's maritime heritage. Kids can try out the moving deck, which simulates what it's like being on board a ship, while the Met Office Weather Gallery offers panoramic views of the Irish Sea. Beaconers sessions – arts and crafts, story-telling and historical re-enactment – are sometimes held.

The town is also worth a wander. Once the third-largest port in England, it retains its Georgian architecture. Also see the Rum Story (see page 158).

Lake District Coast Aquarium

Maryport, CA15 8AB, T01900-817760, lakedistrict-coastaquarium.co.uk. Year round daily 1000-1700, £6.75 adult, £4.50 child, £18.75 family.

Rays, cuttlefish, conger eels, seahorses. You name it, if you're after all things fishy on the west coast, then this is the place. Newly extended to house an exhibition centre and audio-visual lounge, the aquarium is a brilliant resource for children and an excellent wet-weather day out. Aside from the impressive array of tanks with *Finding Nemo*-like species of all sizes and colours, there are plenty of activities to keep kids busy – colouring fish pictures, browsing souvenirs in the shop, or captaining the little boats in the play area. Allow half a day to explore all the attractions and look out for details of the feeding times for a free show.

Muncaster Castle & Gardens

Ravenglass, CA18 1RD, T01229-717614, muncaster.co.uk. Nov-Feb gardens, owl centre and maze daily 1100-1600, castle Sun 1300-1500, £6 adult, £3.50 child, £17 family; Mar-Oct daily 1030-1800 all attractions, £8.50 adult, £6 child (5-15), £27 family.

Muncaster and its extensive grounds are home to myriad attractions for a full family day out and, as such, it is deservedly popular – especially during school holidays. Facilities for families are well thought out, with baby-changing facilities in the toilets and bottle-warming in the cafés. The haunted castle and Himalayan garden are appealing enough, but Muncaster's trump cards are its Owl Centre (T01229-717010, owls.org), where you can meet the owls daily at 1430, and the indoor Meadow Vole Maze, where kids can scurry around a giant wildflower meadow (best for over-fives). There are more than 77 acres of grounds to run around in, including a bluebell wood and a sundial garden, plus a great adventure playground with views across to the castle. Look out for regular events throughout the year, such as the perennially

The Lakeland Sheep & Wool Centre
Nr Cockermouth, CA13 0QX, T01900-822673, sheep-woolcentre.co.uk. Year round 0930-1730, shows £5 adult, £4 child, visitor centre free.

This visitor centre, conveniently located on the A66-A5086 roundabout just south of Cockermouth, is an obvious choice for a rainy day attraction. And it's got a decent café and shop with a woolly theme. But will kids really sit still for a scaled-down take on the rural county show? Well, try to time your visit to catch one of the farm shows (Mar-Oct Sun-Thu at 1030, 1200, 1400 and 1530) and you're onto a winner. The farm show is designed to introduce visitors to different breeds of farm animals, but it actually takes on the atmosphere of a beauty pageant, with the animals parading around like carnival queens. Ewe'll love it.

☻ The hardy hill-breed Herdwick sheep is ideally suited to withstand the harsh Cumbrian winters. With its distinctive white head, grey fleece and sturdy legs, it is difficult to mistake the Herdwick from any other type of sheep. A tup, or 'tip' in the local dialect, is a ram, while a ewe or 'yow' is a female sheep.

popular Festival of Fools in May, Summer of Fun Festival in August and the Halloween Week in October. Older children will enjoy the Darkest Muncaster events in autumn, with late opening across the site, and the ghost tours. Muncaster's most famous ghost, the cheeky jester Tom Fool, often makes an appearance for special events.

☻ Tom Skelton was the court jester at Muncaster in the 1600s, but his penchant for taking his clowning to more sinister ends gave rise to a new word 'tomfoolery'. In May each year Muncaster now hosts a Festival of Fools in honour of his fearsome memory.

Ravenglass & Eskdale Railway
See page 154.

Senhouse Roman Museum
Maryport, CA15 6JD, T01900-816168, senhousemuseum.co.uk. Jul-Oct daily 1000-1700, Nov-Mar Fri-Sun 1030-1600, Apr-Jun Tue, Thu, Fri-Sun 1000-1700, £3 adult, £1 child, £8 family.

If you're heading northwest to explore Hadrian's Wall Country (see page 94), then this educational museum is a good starting point. It's located next to the Roman fort, built in Maryport in the second century AD as part of the Roman Empire's maritime frontier in Britain. There are occasional hands-on sessions in which children can handle some of the artefacts. Pick up a copy of *Humphrey's Guide*, a children's trail around the exhibits, including the chance to dress up as a Roman soldier.

Try to time your visit to Maryport to catch the Roman Festival (entry free), held annually between July and September, when children can march like a Roman centurion.

Wordsworth House and Garden
Cockermouth, CA13 9RX, T01900-824805, wordsworthhouse.org.uk. Apr-Oct Mon-Sat 1100-1700, Feb-Mar weekends only, £5.90 adult, £2.90 child, £14.70 family.

Wordsworth House really does succeed in bringing the poet's

Out & about West Lakes

childhood home to life, even for young children.

Now owned by the National Trust, the house recreates the sights, sounds, noises and clutter of a lively, bustling home in the 18th century. It was saved from dereliction by Wordsworth enthusiasts and restored using records from the Wordsworth archive. Costumed interpreters staff the house in character as servants, while visitors are free to roam the rooms, where clothes are laid out and meals are ready to eat on the table.

The overall effect makes for a much more real experience with no 'Keep Out' signs and lots of interaction with the staff. Visitors are actively encouraged to dress up in period clothes and join in the spirit of the times. Children can follow a trail of wooden animals around the house, then head out into the gardens to explore the wild flowers and

vegetable patches. Look out for special events for families throughout the year, such as an Easter egg trail, Earth Day talks and half-term workshops.

More family favourites

Bank Mill Experience
Beckfoot, nr Silloth-on-Solway, CA7 4LF, T01900-881340, bankmillnurseries.co.uk. Mar-Nov daily 0900-1700, £5 adults, £3 child, £15 family.
Beside the plants, Bank Mill boasts a tropical butterfly house, reptilia and exotic fauna, including a sulphur crested cockatoo and a Bengal eagle owl. There's also a maze, children's play area, picnic area and café.

Eskdale Mill
Boot, Eskdale, CA191TG, T01946-723335, eskdalemill.co.uk. Apr-Sep Tue-Sun 1100-1730 (closed some Sats), £1.50.
This is one of the oldest working mills in Britain, dating from 1578. The entrance fee includes a guided tour by the current miller, who tells stories of the mill's history and valley life in the past. Bring a picnic to enjoy in the grounds afterwards.

Gincase
Silloth, nr Wigton, CA7 4LL, T01697-332020, gincase.co.uk. Easter-Oct daily, Nov-Easter Tue-Sun 1030-1630, £4.50 adult, £3.50 child, £14 family.
This award-winning tearoom and craft gallery make for a one-stop shop, but it's the farm park with resident animals (goats, hens, ducks, geese, pigs, and Shetland ponies) and children's play area with pedal-karts that make it a hit with children.

Kinetic clock, Rum Story café, Whitehaven.

Visit The Rum Story, Whitehaven

Why? This compelling little museum has enough tales of pirates, smugglers, gangsters and Admiral Lord Nelson to keep children captivated. Converted from the town's 18th-century cellars and warehouses, the three-level museum traces a journey from the origins of Whitehaven's dark trade in slaves in the villages of Africa to the Antiguan sugar plantations, and on to the glory days of Whitehaven as a major British port. Along the way are cameos from Blackbeard, the Jazz Age and Nelson's navy.

Where? 27 Lowther Street, Whitehaven, CA28 7DN. Take the A595 to Whitehaven and follow signs for the town centre. A handy little café is an added attraction (see page 170).

How? Year round 1000-1630, £5.45 adult, £3.45 child, £16.45 family.

Contact The Rum Story, T01946-592933, rumstory.co.uk.

Rain check

Arts centres
• **Carnegie Theatre and Arts Centre**
Workington, T01900-602122,
carnegietheatre.co.uk.
• **Kirkgate Arts Centre**
Cockermouth, T01900-826448,
thekirkgate.com.
• **Rosehill Theatre**
Whitehaven, T01946-692422,
rosehilltheatre.co.uk.
• **The Wave Centre**
Maryport, T01900-811450,
thewavemaryport.co.uk.

Arts & crafts
• **Gosforth Pottery**
Gosforth, CA20 1AH, T01946-
725296, potterycourses.co.uk.
During school holidays it runs daily
drop-in sessions on painting pots
(1400-1700).

Bowling
• **Eclipse Tenpin Bowling**
Workington, T01900-872207,
eclipse-bowling.co.uk.

Cinemas
Plaza Cinemas
Workington, CA14 1NQ, T01900-
870001, workington-plaza.co.uk.

Indoor play & amusements
• **Billy Bear's Fun Centre**
Whitehaven, CA28 9AN,
T01946-690003.
• **Clown-A-Round**
Maryport, CA15 6LW,
T01900-818811.

Indoor swimming pools
• **Cockermouth Leisure Centre**
Pool & Climbing Wall, Cockermouth,
CA13 9JR, T01900-823596,
carlisleleisure.com.
• **Netherhall Community Sports
Centre**
Maryport, CA15 6NT,
T01900-812161.
• **Silloth Community Sports Centre**
Silloth, CA7 4DD, T01697-331234.
• **Spring Lea Leisure Centre**
Allonby, nr Maryport, CA15 6QF,
T01900-881331, springlea.co.uk.
• **Whitehaven Sports Centre**
Whitehaven, CA28 7RJ, T01946-
695666.

The Wave Centre, Maryport.

Off the beaten track

Solway Coast

Most visitors to the Lake District rarely make it this far, but for a family seeking peace, nature and a rural escape, this gloriously remote and tranquil part of Cumbria offers a true off-the-beaten track experience. The Solway's outstanding landscapes, diverse habitats and rich heritage were recognized as an Area of Outstanding Natural Beauty (AONB) as long ago as 1964.

But don't go expecting the wealth of facilities of the Central Lakes, or even those of Cockermouth. The Solway Coast is about nature reserves, small villages and a very quiet life. There are no big attractions per se, just lots of space to breathe fresh air and recharge your batteries. Teenagers looking for some local colour will be sorely disappointed.

The area is fringed by the Solway Firth, the narrow estuary separating England and Scotland, characterized by a broad expanse of tidal waters, mudflats and grazed fields. The mudflats and salt marshes are rich feeding grounds for thousands of birds, while the undulating dune grasslands inland are home to many species, including the rare Natterjack toad. The raised peat bogs (or mires) are of international importance for their flora, invertebrates and bird life.

A word of warning: be vigilant in the proximity of open water at all times when exploring the nature reserves. The Solway Coast as a whole is prone to fast-moving tides and quicksand, so don't let children wander off unsupervised.

❷ Peat bogs have been exploited for centuries, mainly as a source of fuel, but large-scale commercial extraction for the horticultural industry in the 1940s caused great damage. Lowland peat bogs are rare habitats, and those on the Solway Plain are protected and managed.

Get your bearings

The AONB stretches from Rockcliffe Marsh, just west of Carlisle, to the sea cliffs north of Maryport, covering an area of some 44 square miles.

It's only accessible by road, from junction 43 of the M6 for Carlisle, then B5307 and B5302 to Silloth. Alternatively, head north from Maryport on the B5300 coast road, hugging the shoreline all the way to Silloth.

The best place to start a visit is the **Solway Coast Discovery Centre** (Silloth, CA7 4DD, T01697-331944, solwaycoastaonb.org.uk, year round Mon-Thu 1000-1600, Fri-Sun 1000-1300 and 1400-1600). The centre has two sections: a tourist information centre for public transport timetables, accommodation bookings and information on attractions, and the Discovery Centre, which has an exhibition (£3.50 adult, £2 child) on the wildlife, heritage, landscape and communities of the Solway Coast. A gallery also features a changing display of artwork by local Solway artists, and there is a craft shop.

Visit the main places of interest

Silloth is the main base for families. It has a range of accommodation, the most popular being **Stanwix Park Holiday Centre** (Silloth, CA7 4HH,

T01697-332666, holidayparkscumbria.co.uk), which has caravans, campers and chalets, plus a swimming pool, ten-pin bowling and laid-on activities for children. Lots of families barely leave the site during their stay.

Skinburness was the principal town on the Solway coast until the early 14th century, but is little more than an extension to Silloth today. **Bowness-on-Solway**, a quiet village with no real accommodation options for families, was founded on the Roman fort of Maia, marking the western end of Hadrian's Wall, the 73-mile frontier between Bowness-on-Solway and Wallsend (Tynemouth), which marked the northern extent of the Roman Empire in Britain.

Although the wall is no longer visible in this area (much of the stone was re-used in later

---

❷ In 1626 Scottish raiders stole the bells of St Michael's Church in Bowness. They jettisoned them in the Solway whilst being pursued back to Scotland. Bowness villagers retaliated by taking the bells from churches in Dumfriesshire, where they are kept at the rear of the church to this day.

buildings), the straight roads still hint of the Roman occupation. The Banks area of Bowness marks the official start (or end) of the Hadrian's Wall Path National Trail.

Explore a nature reserve

A visit to the Solway Coast is all about connecting with nature, so a trip to one of the local nature reserves is the quintessential way to get a feel for the region. Be aware that the reserves are not supervised by staff. In fact, you'll often be the only people there.

Four good reserves for families are:

---

❷ In 1869 the Solway Viaduct was built to link England and Scotland by rail. At the time it was the longest bridge in Europe. After severe storm damage during the winter of 1881, the railway track was abandoned and the viaduct was only occasionally used by Scots visiting the alehouses of Bowness on 'dry' Sundays in Scotland. All that remains today are the two ends of the viaduct projecting into the Solway.

Finglandrigg Wood National Nature Reserve

Eight miles west of Carlisle, off the B5307, this fascinating environment of woodland, peat bog, heathland and rough pasture provides a diverse range of habitats. There are two way-marked routes to follow through the reserve, plus interpretive panels and picnic tables. Children can follow a wood-carving trail through the woods; the designs are carved into the trees. There are parking and cycle racks in the lay-by on the B5307. More information, naturalengland.org.uk.

Campfield Marsh Nature Reserve

Adjoining the Solway Mosses near Bowness-on-Solway, this RSPB reserve of mudflats, salt marshes and raised bogs attracts dragonflies, farmland birds and lots of different waterfowl, including all kinds of ducks – wigeon (reddish head and white forehead), goldeneye (a black and white diving duck), red-breasted merganser (long thin bill and tufted head) and pintail (strikingly marked brown and white duck with a white forehead and a long tail). For children keen on bird watching, North Plain Farm on the reserve has a free-to-use bird hide to watch the local species in their natural habitat. Park at North Plain Farm, Bowness-on-Solway, CA7 5AG. More information, rspb.org.uk.

Bowness-on-Solway Nature Reserve
Located close to Campfield Marsh (see above), this former gravel extraction site of ponds and wetlands has a circular walk, partly on a boardwalk that is suitable for pushchairs. It takes in the pools and passes through flower-rich grasslands. There is limited parking on the grass verge at the entrance to the reserve. More information, cumbriawildlifetrust.org.uk.

South Solway Mosses National Nature Reserve
The reserve comprises four of the best remaining peat bogs in Europe, all under

Grab a bite
Some places to look out for on your travels are: the **Silloth Café** (Silloth, T01697-331319) which has light snacks; the **Golf Hotel** (Silloth, T01697-331438, golfhotelsilloth.co.uk) for bar meals and morning coffees; the **Kings Arms** (Bowness-on-Solway, T01697-351426) for real ales and Sunday lunches; and **Dunes Bistro** (Bank Mill, nr Beckfoot, T01900-881340), good for hearty evening meals Wednesday to Sunday.

Essential websites
solwaycoastaonb.org.uk
western-lakedistrict.co.uk

❷ Silloth gets its name from 'sea lathes', a reference to the time when the Cistercian monks of Holm Cultram Abbey stored their grain in barns, known as 'lathes'.

careful management to encourage the growth of the peat-forming sphagnum mosses. Of the group, Wedholme Flow is the most accessible (take the A596, Kirkbride to Wigton road then an unmarked road heading north), where there are cycle racks, a car park, picnic tables and way-marked trails. More information, cumbriawildlifetrust.org.uk.

Sleeping West Lakes

Dalegarth Guesthouse & Campsite

Buttermere, nr Cockermouth, CA13 9XA, T01768-770233, dalegarthguesthouse.co.uk. Mar-Oct £5.50 adult, £2.50 child, £2.50/vehicle.

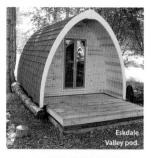

Rural, rustic with no frills, the Dalegarth site – with its accompanying guesthouse if the weather sets in – is a peaceful retreat on the shores of Lake Buttermere. The 35-pitch site has a woodland setting and is laid out across four flat terraces. There is a lockable garage for bikes. Children will love the feeling of being close to nature; there's lots of birdlife around the lake and potential close encounters with deer, foxes and badgers if you don't zip up the tent firmly at night.

Fisherground Campsite

Eskdale Green, Eskdale Valley, CA19 1TF, T01946-723349, fishergroundcampsite.co.uk. Mar-Oct £5.50 adult, £2.50 child, £2.50/vehicle.

A campsite with a play area is always a bonus for kids. And one that allows campfires is a guaranteed hit. But just imagine a campsite that not only holds the promise of marshmallow-toasting, but also boasts a rafting pond, tree house, zip wire, adventure course and a

halt on the Ravenglass & Eskdale Railway (see page 154). Welcome to Fisherground, a children's paradise. The camping facilities are nothing to shout about – there's a toilet block, laundry and boot-drying room – and you can buy logs for the fire.

Hollins Farm Campsite

Boot, Eskdale Valley, CA19 1TF, T01946-723253, hollinsfarmcampsite.co.uk. Year round from £7.25-8.35 adult, £2.50-2.60 child, £19.80-20.65 family, £38/ camping pods.

A rural and quiet site, Hollins Farm was made for families. Set amongst rolling hills and shrouded with tall pine trees, it's a back-to-nature place with good facilities, a small children's play area and a set of new camping pods for that glamping experience. The Brook House Inn (T01946-723288,

brookhouseinn.co.uk), a friendly local pub for bar meals, is just a short stroll from the site.

Also recommended
Barn Door Campsite

Wasdale Head, T01946-726384. Simple campsite with an adjoining shop – the only one around for miles.

High Wallabarrow Camping Barn

Nr Ulpha, Duddon Valley, T01229-715011, wallabarrow.co.uk.

Eskdale Valley pod.

Mackerel for breakfast.

Seacote Caravan Park

St Bees, nr Whitehaven,
T01946-822777, seacote.com.

Tanglewood Caravan Park

Causeway Head, Silloth-
on-Solway, T01697-331253,
tanglewoodcaravanpark.co.uk.

Turner Hall Farm

Nr Seathwaite, Eskdale, T01229-
716420, turnerhall@ktdinternet.com.

Best of the rest

Muncaster Country Guest House

Ravensglass, CA18
1RD, T01229-717693,
muncastercountryguesthouse.com.
£65/double, £75 family plus £15
child sharing, £5 under-2s.
Situated opposite the main
gates to Muncaster Castle
and Gardens (see page 156), this
homely B&B offers comfortable
rooms and a friendly welcome.
The owners will provide evening
meals during the week and
serve up a fine breakfast. Best of
all, the attractions of the castle
are just across the road, making
it perfect for a weekend escape.

Wasdale Head Inn

Wasdale Head, nr Gosforth, CA20
1EX, T01946-726229, wasdale.com.
From £59 pp/B&B hotel rooms (£15
child sharing), from £280 3-night
break/self-catering cottages Nov-
Mar (£440 Apr-Oct).
A little piece of living history, the
Wasdale Head is the birthplace

Playground, Muncaster Castle.

of British mountaineering. It is
also in a jaw-dropping location,
ensuring the remote Wasdale
Head Inn features on all the best
itineraries. Of the nine bedrooms
in the main hotel one has single
beds for a family or group of
siblings sharing, while the six
self-catering apartments in the
separate converted barn include
a couple of family suites for four
people. Recently refurbished,
with an in-house microbrewery
and top-notch pub grub –
what's not to like?

Also recommended The Coachman's Quarters and Muncaster Castle Holiday Cottages

Muncaster Castle, Ravensglass, CA18
1RQ, T01229-717614, muncaster.co.uk.
This four-star B&B within the
grounds of Muncaster Castle
(see page 156) has 10 rooms,
while the three Georgian holiday

cottages, located in nearby
Ravensglass, offer all mod cons
for a self-catering break. Call
ahead for promotional rates in
the low season.

Eskdale YHA

Boot, Eskdale Valley, CA19 1TH,
T0845-371 9317, yha.org.uk.
For easy access to the
Ravensglass & Eskdale Railway
and great walking, this lively,
modern hostel is hard to beat.
It has a good kitchen and bike
hire is available.

Six Castlegate

Cockermouth, CA13 9EU, T01900-
826749, sixcastlegate.co.uk.
A stylish Georgian property
converted into a contemporary
B&B with high-end facilities and
a stylish finish. Make time for
the hearty breakfast, combining
healthy options with locally
sourced meats.

Sleeping West Lakes

Stanley Ghyll

Nr Boot, Eskdale Valley, CA19 1TF, T019467-23327, stanleyghyll-eskdale.co.uk.

A smart, modern B&B in a converted period property. There are two bedroom suites suited to families. It also has rooms that are dog friendly.

Ravenglass & Eskdale Railway Pullman Holiday Coaches

Ravenglass, CA18 1SW, T01229-717171, ravenglass-railway.co.uk. Mar-Oct from £250/week low season, £370/week high season (sleeps 6).

What is a trainspotter's dream holiday home? One which is a custom-fitted Pullman carriage on the doorstep of a heritage railway, of course. Originally built as ambulance cars in the First World War, the two coaches accommodate up to six people in three bedrooms. It's not exactly five-star accommodation – bunk beds and cold-water washbasins in each room – but there are storage heaters and a hot shower. Besides, it's the elegance of yesteryear, not modern trappings, that you'll be after. Guests can also claim reduced fares on the railway and reduced entrance to nearby Muncaster Castle (see page 156).

The Derwent Lodge

Embleton, Bassenthwaite Lake, nr Cockermouth, CA13 9YA, T01768-776606, thederwentlodge.co.uk. From £170-290/self-catering apartments; from £125 room/B&B.

Located just off the A66, between the market towns of Cockermouth and Keswick, the Derwent Lodge is an 18th-century farmhouse with a mix of accommodation. It offers regular B&B but, more interesting for families, a range of self-contained family apartments with top-notch facilities and panoramic views across the fells. The Rydal apartment sleeps

three, while Bassenthwaite sleeps eight. The swimming pool is a new addition.

Glenfield Guest House

Whitehaven, CA28 7TS, T 01946-691911, glenfield-whitehaven.co.uk. Doubles from £60 room/B&B, £65 family plus £10 child sharing. Friendly and homely, Glenfield is on the edge of up-and-coming Whitehaven, a good base to explore the Western Lakes. It's a traditional B&B with comfortable rooms and a good spread for breakfast. What sets it apart, however, is the welcome from the owners, who, as members of the Wainwright Society, happily share their knowledge about walks in the area, even producing a newsletter with top tips and suggested itineraries.

Also recommended
Lowther House

Whitehaven, CA28 7TY, T 01946-63169, lowtherhouse-whitehaven. com. From £80 room/B&B.

Moresby Hall

Moresby, nr Whitehaven, CA28 6PJ, T 01946-696317, moresbyhall.co.uk.

The Old Ginn House

Great Clifton, Workington, CA14 1TS, T 01900-64616, oldginnhouse.co.uk.

Glenfield Guest House.

Eating West Lakes

Local goodies

Country Cuts Farm Shop

Santon Bridge, nr Holmrook, CA19 1UY, T01946-726256, country-cuts. co.uk. Mon-Sat 1000-1700, Sun 1100-1600.

Country Cuts is an excellent farm shop specializing in locally reared meat. Highlights include succulent mutton, wild venison, rare-breed pork and free-range chicken, plus black pudding, Cumberland sausage and air-dried 'Farma' ham.

Millstones

Bootle, nr Millom, LA19 5TJ, T01229-718757, millstonesbootle.co.uk. Tue-Sun 1000-1730.

The Millstones comprises a rustic wood-beamed restaurant, food hall and bakery. In summer, the Byre Restaurant serves home-made lunches on the sunny terrace with coast fell views. The Food Hall, meanwhile, specializes in local cooked meats

and cheeses, and the open-kitchen bakery has mouths drooling with wafts of fresh bread, cakes and pies, using organic stone-ground floor from the Watermill at Little Salkeld (see page 108).

Twentyman's Ice Cream

Allonby, nr Maryport, CA15 6PE, T01900-881247. Summer 0900-2000, winter 1000-1700.

Twentyman's unassuming little general store and ice cream parlour has been a feature of Allonby's seafront since 1920. People come from far and wide for the home-made ice creams and delicious rum butter.

⊖ Solway has the largest brown shrimp fishery on the west coast of the UK. Potted shrimps, the local delicacy, are available from Ray's Shrimps (T016973-31215, raysshrimpsltd.co.uk) and Lomas Fishmongers (T01697-331334), both in Silloth.

Wasdale Fell Meats

Wasdale Head, nr Seascale, CA20 1EX, T01946-726245, wasdalefellmeats.com. Summer daily 0930-1830, winter – call for hours.

A superb local farm shop to stock up on Herdwick lamb and mutton, Galloway and Angus beef and free-range eggs.

Wellington Farm

Cockermouth, CA13 0QU, T01900-822777, wellingtonjerseys.co.uk. Year round daily 1000-1700, hot food 1130-1430.

Wellington, a rustic farm in the Stamper family since 1946, has built an empire around its herd of pedigree Jerseys. It has an ice cream parlour, tea rooms and a farm shop. The ice cream comes in 16 flavours, including whisky and marmalade. After tucking in, check out the farm trail around Dubbs Moss, a wetland area rich in wildlife – bring your wellies.

Also recommended
Greens of Millom

Millom, T01229-772466. A traditional bakers and confectioners.

Lake District Creamery

Aspatria, nr Wigton, T01697-320218, lakedistrictcheesecompany.co.uk.

Teddy bear cones, Twentyman's Ice Cream.

Market days

Workington Wednesday and Saturday
Cockermouth First Saturday
Whitehaven Thursday & Saturday

The Vagabond,
Whitehaven harbour.

Uses the milk from local dairy farms to produce premium quality cheeses.

Whins Farm Shop

Workington, T01946-830373.
A good range of Cumbrian products, including local honey, milk and cheese, as well as the farm's own beef and lamb.

Quick & simple

The Bridge Inn

Santon Bridge, nr Holmrook, CA19 1UX, T01946-726221, santonbridgeinn.com.
The Bridge Inn is a welcoming spot in the Wasdale Valley for home-cooked local produce. There is a popular Sunday carvery and on other days a host of hearty mains for lunch and dinner. Try the Lamb Jennings (£13.95), a large shoulder of lamb marinated in Jennings Lakeland Bitter, served with creamy mashed potato and a selection of vegetables.

Merienda

Cockermouth, CA3 9QU, T01900-822790, merienda.co.uk. Mon-Sat 0900-1700.
A cosy and friendly little café in the heart of bustling Cockermouth, Merienda serves the best espresso in the Western Lakes, tasty lunches (mains around £4) and scrummy afternoon teas. There are nappy-changing facilities and a kids' menu, including a boiled egg and soldiers (£2.25) and kids' triple sandwiches (£2.95). The café also hosts occasional live music events on Friday evenings.

The Vagabond

Whitehaven, CA28 7LL, T01946-693671, myspace.com/thevagabondwhitehaven.
The Vagabond, a hearty local gastropub for hearty pub grub (mains £9-14) and real ales, is a welcome addition to Whitehaven's burgeoning dining scene. Try to sit upstairs

Liar!

The Bridge Inn (Santon Bridge, nr Holmrook, CA19 1UX, T01946-726221, santonbridgeinn.com) is almost as famous for its good food and local produce as for its porky-telling championship, the World's Biggest Liar competition.

The event, held annually in November, dates back to the 19th century when the pub landlord, Will Ritson, kept his customers enthralled with extraordinary stories of local folklore.

One of his favourite yarns revolved around the claim that the turnips in Wasdale were so big that, after the dales folk had 'quarried' into them for their Sunday lunch, they could be used as sheds for the Herdwick sheep from the fells.

These days the contest awards the title of 'The Biggest Liar in the World' to the person who is worthy of following in the footsteps of Auld Will. Participants have up to five minutes to tell the biggest and most convincing lie they can, without the aid of props.

The contest attracts entrants from as far afield as South Africa and New Zealand. A recent winner was the comedian Sue Perkins, who won the contest with a tale of flatulent sheep causing a hole in the ozone layer.

She also made a programme about her attempts to steal the crown from the local entrants for BBC Radio 4.

Eating West Lakes

to catch the sunset from the bay windows overlooking the harbour. The only downside is that it can get very busy and service can therefore be slow. Best to get here early, bag a good table and order your food before the rush.

Fish & chips

The pick of the chips is **Crosby's** (Whitehaven, T01946-62622), while **Main Street Fisheries** (Cockermouth, T01900-828448) is also worth a try. The **Allonby Fish & Chip Shop** (Allonby, T01900-881436) is a multi-purpose spot for a fish supper, your daily newspaper and essential groceries. Check out the latter's Big Yan breakfast – a gut-busting blow out for £4.99.

Also recommended
The Courtyard Café,
The Rum Story
Whitehaven, T01946-592933, rumstory.co.uk.
A handy little café built around the Rum Story's kinetic clock, which clatters and whirrs into life every hour. Hot food daily 1130-1545 and coffees at other times. Mains around £5.

Fellbites Café
Dalegarth Station and Visitor Centre, Boot, CA19 1TF, T01946-723192, ravenglass-railway.co.uk.
Visiting Eskdale on the Ravensdale and Eskdale Railway? Then stop off for a cuppa and a home-made snack at this cosy little café in the station. Kids' options are also available. See page 154 for more on the railway.

Jordans Jungle Funhouse
Cockermouth, T01900-826115.
A café with an indoor soft play area suitable for ages two to 11. Also holds parents and toddler mornings Monday and Friday 0930-1130.

Ratty Arms
Ravenglass, CA18 1SN, T01229-717676.
An atmospheric pub overlooking the platform at Ravenglass train station, home of La'al Ratty. It boasts lots of railway memorabilia for the hungry trainspotter. It offers home-made pub grub, an open fire in winter and a large patio in summer.

Posh nosh

Zest Harbourside
Cockermouth, CA28 7LR, T01946-66981, zestwhitehaven.com/harbourside.aspx. Mon-Sat 1100-2300, Sun 1100-2230.
The sister venue to high-end eatery Zest (located just out of town, on the B5345 towards St Bees) is suited to families in search of top tucker. It's a family-friendly open-plan place with a lounge area and a large menu. Try the locally caught fish mains (around £8) or a lighter bite, such as salads and sandwiches (around £6). And ask about the menu of weekly changing specials. Dogs are welcome too.

Also recommended
Quince & Medlar
Cockermouth, CA13 9EU, T01900-823579, quinceandmedlar.co.uk.
Tue-Sat dinner only.
This is a stylish and award-winning vegetarian and organic restaurant with an inspiring menu – even for non-vegetarians. Best suited to sophisticated older children.

Tarantella
Cockermouth, CA13 9LQ, T01900-822109, tarantellarestaurant.co.uk.
Tue-Fri 1730-2200, Sat 1800-2200.
This is a high-end Italian restaurant; sister property to the Ambleside original.

Cheese for sale.

Grown-ups' stuff Lake District

Getting there

By car Coming by car? Then make the M6 your friend. It's the main artery to the Lakes, running along the eastern fringe of the national park. The bottleneck junctions are 36 for the A590 South Lakes road, 37 for the A591 Windermere road, which dissects the National Park, and 40 for the A66 Penrith to Cockermouth road via Keswick. For Carlisle, exit at junction 43. Expect queues at peak times.

In the far west, the A595 and A596 are the main coast roads. While these are quieter, you should expect slow going due to farm machinery and tight bends. And tune into BBC Radio Cumbria (see page 182) for traffic information while you're behind the wheel.

In terms of journey times, count on a five-hour drive or so from London (break on the M6 around Birmingham), 90 minutes from Liverpool or Manchester (break at Tebay) and two hours from Edinburgh or Glasgow (break at Gretna Green).

For navigation, Sat Nav will only get you so far – especially in the rural areas. The AA (theaa.com) *Road Atlas to Great Britain and Ireland* will serve you well, even if you're heading off the beaten track.

The best service station in Cumbria – and probably in the UK – is Tebay, at junction 38 of the M6 (see page 102).

By coach National Express (nationalexpress.com) serves Ambleside, Carlisle, Grasmere, Kendal, Keswick, Penrith, Ulverston and Windermere.

By train West Coast Main Line services, calling at Carlisle, Penrith and Oxenholme, are operated by Virgin Trains (virgintrains.co.uk). First TransPennine Express (tpexpress.co.uk) runs trains from Manchester Airport (the nearest airport to the Lakes) to Oxenholme, Penrith and Carlisle.

❸ Each year over 15 million visitors to Cumbria contribute more than £1 billion to the local economy and support around 30% of local jobs in tourism.

First TransPennine Express also runs the Lakes Line from Oxenholme to Windermere, and part of the Furness Line between Lancaster and Barrow-in-Furness via Arnside and Ulverston.

Northern Rail (northernrail. org) operates both the supremely scenic Settle–Carlisle Line from Lancaster to Carlisle and the Cumbrian Coast Line from Barrow-in-Furness to Carlisle via Ravenglass, Whitehaven and Maryport.

More service details from National Rail Enquiries (T0845-748 4950, nationalrail.co.uk).

The Settle to Carlisle railway (settle-carlisle.co.uk), the Tyne Valley cross-country route to Newcastle, and the Cumbrian Coast Railway to Barrow-in-Furness meet at Carlisle's Citadel Station, the regional rail hub.

There are several value-for-money rail tickets available, including the Cumbrian Coast Day Ranger ticket which is valid for one day's travel, while the Cumbria Round Robin ticket is valid for a circular journey in any direction on any one day; more details from northernrail.org.

Getting around

By boat See page 44 for services on Coniston Water, Derwentwater and Windermere; for Ullswater, see page 93. Also look at the possibilities of linking

up with other forms of transport (see box above).

By bus Stagecoach Cumbria (stagecoachbus.com) operates a network of rambler bus services, including the following routes:
77 Keswick–Portinscale–Grange–Seatoller–Honister Slate Mine–Buttermere–Whinlatter Forest Visitor Centre–Keswick.
108 Penrith–Pooley Bridge–Aira Force–Glenridding–Patterdale.
505 Kendal–Windermere–Ambleside–Hawkshead (for Tarn Hows)–Waterhead (for Coniston boat services)–Coniston.

Grown-ups' stuff Lake District

516 Ambleside–Skelwith Bridge–Elterwater–Chapel Stile–Dungeon Ghyll. The 505 carries bikes free of charge, but there's only space for two bikes so book ahead: T01539-472 2143.
517 Bowness Pier–Windermere–Kirkstone Pass–Brothers Water–Patterdale–Glenridding.
555 Kendal–Windermere–Brockhole National Park Centre–Ambleside–Grasmere–Keswick.

The **Hadrian's Wall Bus** (AD 122) operates along the course of the Wall (Easter-Oct) and can carry up to two bicycles free of charge; timetables and other information from nationaltrail.co.uk/hadrianswall.

North West Explorer tickets allow travel on all Stagecoach buses (stagecoachbus.com) in Cumbria and Lancashire; tickets can be purchased on any Stagecoach service.

Cumbria Goldrider allows unlimited travel anywhere within Cumbria on any Stagecoach service over seven or 28 days. Tickets from Stagecoach, travel shops and some tourist information centres.

By car If you don't want the hassle of driving to the Lake District but like the independence a car provides while you are there, consider

hiring one in situ. Carlisle railway station has branches of the national car rental chains.

By train Scenic steam railway routes include the Lakeside & Haverthwaite and Ravenglass & Eskdale (see pages 55 and 154).

Travel enquiry line
T0871-200 2233, traveline.info.

Specialist tours
Lake District Tours
T01539-552106, lakedistricttours.co.uk.
Half-day and full-day sightseeing tours, with an emphasis on nature and hiking.

Scandale above Ambleside.

Cottages &
holiday parks

Cottage agents
Coniston Country Cottages
conistoncottages.co.uk.
Coppermines Mountain
Cottages coppermines.co.uk.
Cumbrian Cottages
cumbrian-cottages.co.uk.
Heart of the Lakes
heartofthelakes.co.uk.
Keswick Cottages
keswickcottages.co.uk.
Lake District Inns & Cottages
lakedistrictinns.co.uk.
Lakeland Cottage Holidays
lakelandcottages.co.uk.
Lakeland Hideaways
lakeland-hideaways.co.uk.
Lakelovers
lakelovers.co.uk.
National Trust Cottages
nationaltrustcottages.co.uk.
Windermere Lake Cottages
lakewindermere.net.

Holiday parks
Lakeland Leisure Park
lakeland-park.co.uk
Lowther Holiday Park
lowther-holidaypark.co.uk.
Stanwix Park
stanwix.com
Wild Rose Park
wildrose.co.uk

Lakes Supertours
T 01539-442751, lakes-supertours.com.
Specializes in half-day and
full-day tours in small 16-seater
mini-coaches, including literary
tours taking in sites associated
with Wordsworth, Ruskin, Beatrix
Potter and Arthur Ransome.

Mountain Goat
T 01539-445161, mountain-goat.com.
Provides holidays and half- and
full-day sightseeing tours of the
Lake District. Itineraries include
the Beatrix Potter Experience,
a short break focusing on the
various locations associated with
Potter's life and stories.

Podcast tours
Cumbria Tourism has produced
a series of eight podcasts of
classic Lake District walks based
on those devised by Alfred
Wainwright (1907-1991), the
fell walker who opened up the
Lakeland fells to thousands of
amateur explorers. The idea
takes the concept of audio tours
often available in museums
and art galleries and transfers it
to the Lake District. The audio
walks feature the voice of Nik
Wood-Jones, familiar as the
voice of the writer in the BBC's
series *Wainwright Walks*.
The podcasts can be downloaded
from golakes.co.uk/wainwright.

Maps
Ordnance Survey
Explorer maps OL4-7
cover the Lake District.
For more information, see
ordnancesurvey.co.uk.

Grown-ups' stuff Lake District

In many ways Cumbria epitomizes our idea of the great British holiday. It's a place people often first visited as a child and later return to with their own children.

Okay, so you may not have the place to yourself during the summer holidays, but you'll have no problem finding bottle warmers, baby food, high chairs and booster seats. At the other end of the age range, there's also more than enough going on to keep the surliest of teenagers happy.

Grandparents, too, are well catered for, with lots of activities offering cross-generational appeal. Single parents, meanwhile, will find plenty to foster special bonding time and are likely to meet other single-parent families along the way.

The range of accommodation caters to families of all shapes and sizes. Most families will eschew chic bolt holes when the children are small in favour of the wealth of high-quality cottages, holiday parks and self-catering apartments offering a home-from-home experience. Even camping can be cool, with yurts, tipis and camping pods ensuring a comfortable stay whatever the weather. See box, page 175, for a list of cottage agents and holiday parks.

Babies (0-18 months)

Babies will happily soak up the holiday vibe from the comfort of their pushchair in towns like Keswick and Ambleside, while crawling around on the beaches of the west coast or the parks in the northern Lakes offers a chance to stretch growing limbs.

The Central Lakes has the best infrastructure for families with babies, including public transport that can accommodate buggies. But the quieter South Lakes offers a more relaxing break. The traffic is quieter, the cafés less crowded and the South Lakes Animal Park is a great day out for even tiny tots.

And, of course, the big advantage of babies is that you can travel outside school holiday periods, getting better deals and a lot more privacy. Load up the car with all the necessary gear and set off. Babies give you the freedom to tear up the schedule and take your time.

Toddlers/pre-school (18 months-4 years)

Avoiding long car journeys is key to preventing a stand-off with a fractious two-year-old, so book a cottage or a campsite, make your base and plan your excursions accordingly. The Central Lakes will most likely be your target area due to its wealth of attractions, but the West Lakes, with its beaches, is another good option.

The facilities at many of the campsites across the region, such as the award-winning Castlerigg Hall Caravan and Camping Park, Keswick (see page 64), are oriented towards young children, with play areas and a plethora of facilities. Many are situated close to towns or villages, making it an easy stroll in search of ice creams and sticker books.

Cottages have the twin advantages of being a new place to explore and a home from home, thus not disrupting the normal routine too much.

The ever-curious minds of toddlers will be inspired by attractions such as Walby Farm Park (see page 101) and Trotters World of Animals (see page 59), which provide perfect introductions to nature and wildlife in a safe environment. Indeed, animal attractions form a big part of the Lakes' appeal to pre-school visitors.

Kids (4-12 years)

Once children start school a raft of new options opens up for the family break. From a gentle climb up Catbells (see page 48) to a cruise on the steam yacht *Gondola* on Coniston (see page 44) or an easy biking or hiking trail in Grizedale Forest Park (see page 38), there are plenty of options to broaden young horizons. Camping or self-catering cottages still tend to be the preferred choice of accommodation for most families with children of this age, but with greater mobility you can strike out further and explore more widely.

This age group is also ready to delve into a little local history, food and culture, making the North Lakes a good choice. Options here include a kids' cooking class at Augill Castle. You can also delve into the flora and fauna of the region with walks around the lakes, biking trails through the forest or a nature ramble around a country estate. Brantwood, for example, may seem like a boring old house to a younger child, but its gardens are full of exciting nooks and crannies and a great place to run wild.

As the children grow older and become more involved in the National Curriculum, you can even make a head start on next year's course work. Engender an early interest in literature with a visit to Dove Cottage, or re-enact a scene from Roman history at Birdoswald Roman Fort near Brampton. Don't miss a walk along Hadrian's Wall.

Teenagers (13 years+)
By the teenage years, offspring are often keener to make their own way than tag along with mum and dad. But the Lakes are a productive setting for the kind of family-bonding moments that turn into golden memories once they leave the nest.

This is the age to start appreciating the finer things in life, so smart hotels and great food are back on the agenda – much to the relief of parents. Even a truculent teen will like the idea of rubbing shoulders with minor celebrities in a cool hotel dining room. And if you decide to hire one of the roomier cottages available, there may be enough space for them to bring a friend from school.

Besides, the Lakes is not without its fashionable side. There are great shopping opportunities for teenagers in towns like Penrith and Cockermouth, while the many outdoor activities on offer will satisfy teenagers looking for an adrenaline-fuelled escape.

Evening options, too, open up at this age – and we don't just mean dodgy nightclubs. The Brewery Arts Centre in Kendal is a haven for live gigs and arthouse films, while Zeffirellis in Ambleside offers a great pizza-and-film combo.

Teenagers may find the West and South Lakes a little quiet for their liking, but the North and Central Lakes will win over the most moody of teens.

Special needs
The Lake District National Park Authority (lake-district.gov. uk) has road-tested a series of wheelchair-accessible routes for people with limited mobility as part of the Miles Without

Stiles project (lakedistrict.gov. uk/index/visiting/outdoors/ mileswithoutstiles.htm). This makes some walking trails, such as the Grasmere River Path and Buttermere shoreline, accessible to wheelchair users.

Another excellent resource is the Lake District Visitor Centre at Brockhole (T01539-446601, lake-district.gov.uk), which offers wheelchairs for use inside the building, electric wheelchairs to explore the gardens and a shuttle bus to transport visitors from the car park to the reception. See page 32.

Single parents
As in most regions, special deals for families – family room rates and family tickets at attractions – are invariably based upon the two-adults-two children model. The best advice for single parents looking to keep costs down is to stick to the smaller, family-run B&Bs, where rates are often worked out by room rather than the number of people. Becoming a member of the National Trust or English Heritage, both of which offer discounted or free entry to the attractions that they run, can also be a smart move.

Campsites, youth hostels and places with communal dining facilities, such as the excellent Augill Castle near Kirkby Stephen (see page 106) are good places to mix with other family groups of all descriptions.

Evening fire at
the YHA Centre,
Windermere.

Grown-ups' stuff Lake District

Essentials

Local knowledge

In the North and Central Lakes, the extensive infrastructure ensures all eventualities are met. Main towns such as Carlisle, Penrith and Bowness-on-Windermere are ideal for stocking up on supplies and browsing for local specialities, with supermarkets, pharmacies and gift shops aplenty. Penrith has numerous independent shops for toys and kids' clothes. The infrastructure is a bit thinner in the south and west, but the hub towns of Ulverston, Grange-over-Sands, Whitehaven and Cockermouth can fulfil the needs of most visitors.

In particular, look out for Booths (T01772-693800, booths-supermarkets.co.uk), a regional group of well-stocked supermarkets with outlets in Kendal, Keswick, Kirkby Lonsdale, Ulverston and Windermere.

The following is a list of main services and facilities.

Hospitals & health

For minor accidents go to the casualty department of the nearest hospital (listed below). For other enquiries phone NHS Direct 24-hours (T0845-4647, nhsdirect.nhs.uk) for advice.

Local hospitals and clinics
Cumberland Infirmary Carlisle, CA2 7HY, T01228-523444.
Cottage Hospital Cockermouth, CA13 9HT, T1900-822226.
Furness General Hospital Barrow-in-Furness, LA14 4LF, T01229-870870.
Grange Clinic Grange-over-Sands, LA11 6BE, T01539-536980.
Penrith Hospital Penrith, CA11 8HX, T01768-245300.
Ulverston Community Health Centre Ulverston, LA12 7BT, T01229-484040.
West Cumberland Hospital Whitehaven, CA28 8JG , T01946-693181.
Westmorland General Kendal, LA9 7RG, T01539-732288.

Pharmacies
Ambleside Boots, Market Cross.
Hawkshead Collins & Butterworth, Main St.
Kendal Asda, Burton Rd.
Keswick Boots/Co-op, Main St.
Penrith Co-op, Middlegate.
Windermere Windermere Health Centre, Goodly Dale.

Supermarkets
Carlisle Tesco Metro.
Cockermouth Sainsbury's.
Dalton-in-Furness Asda.
Kendal Asda, Booths, Morrison.
Keswick Booths.
Penrith Morrison, Somerfield.
Ulverston Tesco Metro.
Windermere Booths.

Right: Goods for sale at Keswick Market.

Farmers' markets

Brampton Moot Hall, last Saturday of month, 0930-1330.
Brough Memorial Hall, third Saturday of month, 0930-1400.
Carlisle city centre, first Friday of month, 0930-1530.
Cockermouth Market Place, first Saturday of month, 0930-1400.
Hadrian's Wall Farmers' Market Greenhead Village Hall, second Sunday of month, 1000-1400.
Kendal Market Place, last Friday of month, 0930-1530.
Penrith Market Square, third Tuesday of month, 0900-1430.
Sedbergh Joss Lane Car Park, last Wednesday of month, 0900-1430.
Ulverston New Market St, third Saturday of month, 0930-1430.
Whitehaven Market Place, second Saturday of month, 1000-1500.

Local brews

Academy Ale from the Tirril Brewery.
Bluebird Bitter from the Coniston Brewing Co.
Celebration Ale from the Ulverston Brewing Company.
Damson Beer from the Masons Arms, Cartmel Fell.
Ennerdale Copper from the Ennerdale Brewery.
Golden Fleece from the Dent Brewery.
Jennings Cocker Hoop from the Jennings Brewery.
Lakeland Gold from the Hawkshead Brewery.

Jennings Brewery.

Grown-ups' stuff Lake District

Tag Lag from the Barngates Brewery.
Thirst Run from the Keswick Brewing Company.

Tourist information centres
The official website of Cumbria Tourism is golakes.co.uk.
See page 32 for details of the Lake District Visitor Centre at Brockhole. Overall, Cumbria has an excellent network of official tourist information centres across the region, and there are also some independent tourism centres:
Alston Town Hall, Front St, CA9 3RF, T01434-382244.
Ambleside Central Buildings, Market Cross, LA22 9BS, T01539-432582.
Appleby Moot Hall, Boroughgate, CA16 6XE, T01768-351177.
Barrow Forum 28, Duke St, LA14 1HU, T01229-876505.
Bowness Bay Glebe Rd, Bowness-on-Windermere, LA23 3HJ, T01539-442895.
Brampton Moot Hall, Market Place, CA8 1RW, T01697-73433.
Broughton Old Town Hall, The Square, LA20 6JF, T01229-716115.
Carlisle Old Town Hall, Green Market, CA3 8JD, T01228-625600.
Cockermouth Town Hall, Market Street, CA13 9NP, T01900-822634.
Coniston Ruskin Avenue, LA21 8EH, T01539-441533.

Grange (volunteer-run so opening times may vary), Victoria Hall, Main St, LA11 6DP, T01539-534026.
Hawkshead (independent), Main St, LA22 0NT, T01539-436946.
Kendal Town Hall, Highgate, LA9 4DL, T01539-797516.
Keswick Market Square, CA12 5JR, T01768-772645.
Kirkby Stephen Market St, CA17 4QN, T01768-371199.
Millom Millom Council Centre, St Georges Rd, LA18 4DD, T01946-598914.
Maryport The Wave Tourist Information Centre (independent), Irish St, CA15 8AD, T01900-811450.
Penrith Robinson's School, Middlegate, CA11 7PT, T01768-867466.
Sedbergh 72 Main St, LA10 5AD, T01539-620125.
Silloth Solway Discovery Centre, Liddell St, CA7 4DD, T01697-331944.
Southwaite M6 Service Area, Southwaite, nr Carlisle, CA4 0NS, T01697-473445.
Ullswater Main Car Park, Glenridding, CA11 0PA, T01768-482414.
Ulverston Coronation Hall, County Square, LA12 7LZ, T01229-587120.
Whitehaven Market Hall, Market Place, CA28 7JG, T01946-598914.
Windermere Victoria St, LA23 1AD, T01539-446499.
Workington 21 Finkle St, CA14 2BE, T01900-606699.

National Trust
For details of becoming a member, see page 5.
Membership of the Trust offers a host of benefits, including free entry to a huge array of properties and free parking at over 20 car parks, including popular family walking spots like Aira Force, Buttermere, Elterwater and Tarn Hows.
Six of the best things to do in the Lakes thanks to the Trust are:
• Have afternoon tea at Acorn Bank
• Try the exhilarating new zip wire at Fell Foot Park
• Take an Explorer Cruise on the steam yacht *Gondola*
• See the falls at Aira Force
• Walk around Tarn Howes
• Join a conservation tour at Townend

English Heritage
For details of joining English Heritage, see page 5.
English Heritage properties in the Lake District include, among many others, Ravenglass Roman Bathhouse, parts of Hadrian's Wall, Furness Abbey, Holker Hall and Muncaster Castle.

To take the pulse of the region:
❶ Read the *Westmorland Gazette* westmorlandgazette.co.uk);
❷ Listen to BBC Radio Cumbria (101FM); 3)
❸ Watch Northwest Tonight weekdays at 2225;
❹ Call the Lake District Weatherline (T0870-0550575, lake-district.gov. uk/weatherline).

Index

Image credits

Footprint story

1921

Ireland had just been partitioned, the British miners were striking for more pay and the federation of British industry had an idea. Exports were booming in South America – how about a handbook for businessmen trading in that faraway continent? The Anglo-South American Handbook was born that year, written by W Koebel, the most prolific writer on Latin America of his day.

1924

Two editions later the book was 'privatized' and, in 1924, in the hands of Royal Mail, the steamship company for South America, it became The South American Handbook, subtitled 'South America in a nutshell'. This annual publication became the 'bible' for generations of travellers to South America and remains so to this day. In the early days travel was by sea and the Handbook gave all the details needed for the long journey from Europe. What to wear for dinner; how to arrange a cricket match with the Cable & Wireless staff on the Cape Verde Islands and a full account of the journey from Liverpool Amazon to Manaus: 5898 miles without changing cabin!

1939

As the continent opened up, The South American Handbook reported the new Pan Am flying boat services, and the fortnightly airship service from Rio to Europe on the Graf Zeppelin. For reasons still unclear but with extraordinary determination, the annual editions continued through the Second World War.

1970s

Many more people discovered South America and the backpacking trail strarted to develop. All the while the Handbook was gathering fans, including literary vagabonds such as Paul Theroux and Graham Greene (who once sent some updates addressed to "The publishers of the best travel guide in the world, Bath, England").

1990s

During the 1990s the company set about developing a new travel guide series using this legendary title as the flagship. By 1997 there were over a dozen guides in the series and the Footprint imprint was launched.

2000s

The series grew quickly and there were soon Footprint travel guides covering more than 150 countries. In 2004, Footprint launched its first thematic guide: Surfing Europe, packed with colour photographs, maps and charts. This was followed by further guides such as Diving the World, Snowboarding the World, Body and Soul escapes, Travel with Kids and European City Breaks.

2010

Today we continue the traditions of the last 89 years that has served legions of travellers so well. We believe that these help to make Footprint guides different. Our policy is to use authors who are genuine experts who write for independent travellers; people possessing a spirit of adventure, looking to get off the beaten track.

A slice of Italy

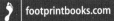

credits

Footprint credits

Project Editor: Jo Williams
Text Editor: Dorothy Stannard
Picture editors: Angus Dawson, Rob Lunn
Proof reader: Catherine Charles
Layout & production: Angus Dawson
Maps: Kevin Feeney

Managing Director: Andy Riddle
Commercial Director: Patrick Dawson
Publisher: Alan Murphy
Publishing managers: Felicity Laughton, Jo Williams
Digital Editor: Alice Jell
Design: Mytton Williams
Marketing: Liz Harper, Hannah Bonnell
Sales: Jeremy Parr
Advertising: Renu Sibal
Finance & administration: Elizabeth Taylor

Print

Manufactured in India by Nutech

Footprint Feedback

We try as hard as we can to make each Footprint guide as up to date as possible but, of course, things always change. If you want to let us know about your experiences – good, bad or ugly – then don't delay, go to footprinttravelguides.com and send in your comments.

Publishing information

Footprint Lake District with Kids, 1st edition
© Footprint Handbooks Ltd, April 2010

ISBN 978-1-906098-98-8
CIP DATA: A catalogue record for this book is available from the British Library

* Footprint Handbooks and the Footprint mark are a registered trademark of Footprint Handbooks Ltd

Published by Footprint

6 Riverside Court
Lower Bristol Road
Bath BA2 3DZ, UK
T +44 (0)1225 469141
F +44 (0)1225 469461
discover@footprinttravelguides.com
footprinttravelguides.com

Distributed in North America by

Globe Pequot Press, Guilford, Connecticut

Ordnance Survey® This product includes mapping data licensed from Ordnance Survey® with the permission of the Controller of Her Majesty's Stationery Office. © Crown Copyright. All rights reserved. Licence No. 100027877.

Acknowledgements

The author would like to offer special thanks to Julie Darroch and Nicola Hewitson at Cumbria Tourism for their valuable advice and support. Thanks also to Neil Atkinson for fresh eyes and a crash course in Roman history, to Christopher Atkinson for his company on drives up and down the M6 and, most importantly, to Maya Atkinson for giving her dad a fresh take on a familiar region.